c·r·e·a·t·i·n·g FAMILY MEMORIES

c·r·e·a·t·i·n·g FAMILY MEMORIES

Brothers

Mark
13 years old

Richard
11 years old

Christopher
9 months

All of us together

Christopher & Mark

Christopher & Richard

April 1987
15 Queens Court
Queens Road
Hertford

CAROLYN SCHULZ & DEBBIE VERTREES

ristopher on wheels

oy could you move with this baby walker!

You loved to bump into the furniture... it made you bounce about!

What shall we do now?

All that whizzing around has made me hungry. Let's eat!

David & Charles

We dedicate this book to our children Mark, Richard, Aaron, Leanne and Christopher who have given us so many wonderful memories through the years. Poring over the multitude of family photographs in preparation for this project has helped us to remember how fortunate we are to have you in our lives. Thank you for your love and support.

A DAVID & CHARLES BOOK

First published in the UK in 1998
Text and photograph album page designs Copyright © Carolyn Schulz 1998
Photography, artwork and layout Copyright © David & Charles 1998

Carolyn Schulz has asserted her right to be identified as author of this work
in accordance with the Copyright, Designs and Patents Act, 1988.
The information given in this book is based on the information currently available at the time of writing. For in-depth
information on photographic conservation procedures, readers should contact a professional archival association or library.

A catalogue record for this book is available from the British Library.

ISBN 0 7153 0828 9

Photography by Alan Duns and Dave Richards
Book design by Diana Knapp
Illustrations by Penny Brown and Diana Knapp

Printed and bound in Great Britain by
Butler & Tanner Ltd, Frome and London
for David & Charles
Brunel House   Newton Abbot   Devon

CONTENTS

$\mathcal{I}$NTRODUCTION

WHAT ARE MEMORY ALBUMS AND WHY ARE SO MANY PEOPLE GETTING CAUGHT UP IN THE ACTIVITY? THEY ARE A CREATIVE AND HIGHLY ENJOYABLE WAY OF PRESERVING MEMORIES THROUGH PHOTOGRAPHS.

$\mathcal{A}$LMOST EVERYONE HAS PHOTOGRAPHS which have been taken to record important events or stages in their lives as well as the lives of family and friends. Most of us start out with good intentions and the record of our early family life can be found organised into an attractive wedding album, a record of our children's baby years and possibly even a few albums of other occasions.

However, most of us find that as our family develops so do the demands on our time and soon we are moving along at such a pace that, while we still manage to take photographs of important events (though not nearly as many as we'd like), these pictures don't get much further than a collection in a box under the bed or at the back of a cupboard.

It is so much more enjoyable to view your collection of photographs if they are mounted and placed in some sort of order, and you'll find family and friends are also more interested in sharing and reliving the memories recorded if they are accessible.

Memory albums are a creative way of preserving memories through photographs and journaling. They provide details which allow you to relive your memories. As modern story books, they provide a history of life that can be enjoyed now and for generations to come.

Putting together a memory album is a unique means of bringing memories to life by using pictures and words to tell a story. By sharing them with others, particularly future generations, we can ensure that these memories won't fade or be forgotten.

Creating a memory album has a way of bringing families together. It can provide a common bond that gives each family member a feeling of belonging, reinforcing the importance of their role within the family. It can also provide individuals with a source of self worth as they relive the experiences through their memories or learn about their ancestry.

Our memories should be cherished and shared. The creation of a memory album captures those precious moments which are an important expression of our lives. They are a priceless possession that should be treasured for generations.

Zermatt Switzerland
Christmas Day
1997

Posing under the Matterhorn

Gornergrat
Sunnega
Kleine Matterhorn

A Perfect Winter Holiday

The · Demons · of · the · Slopes !!

Hotel Nicoletta
Zermatt

Sun, Snow, Speed!

Christopher, Tony & Richard

Everything you...

HAPPY BIRTHDAY

BEN
3

Swimming Lessons 1984
We loved wearing the swim fins!! Reann 4 yrs.

Contents

need to know...

Bryce and Madeline stickers from Melissa Neufeld Inc.© Jone Hallmark. Available from First Class Stamps Ltd.

GETTING STARTED

DON'T YOU JUST LOVE OPENING UP A PACK OF NEWLY DEVELOPED FILM? WHAT FUN IT IS TO PORE OVER THE LATEST PICTURES AND RELIVE EVENTS WHICH WE OBVIOUSLY FELT WERE IMPORTANT ENOUGH TO RECORD. BUT WHAT HAPPENS NEXT?

Do you label up each of your prints and mount them in an album, ready to be enjoyed by family and friends? Or do you add them to the mounting collection in a shoe box at the back of a cupboard or the bottom drawer of an old chest in the spare room, waiting for the chance – when you have the time – to organise and mount them?

Obviously photographs are important to us, or we wouldn't bother to invest time taking pictures or money buying cameras and films and paying for processing. Then why do we find it so hard to get them organised and mounted for future enjoyment?

For many of us, the task is so daunting, we just don't know where to begin, and the longer we leave it, the more impossible it becomes. It is also true that we live very busy lives and there isn't always time to do something that we don't see as an essential task.

While creating a record of your family's memories may not be vital to human survival, it is worth considering the benefits that it offers which can be more important than we realise. Try bringing out a batch of photographs and laying them out on a table. Notice, as you look through them yourself, that family and friends cannot help but stop and reminisce with you.

Re-living memories through photographs is something that appeals to everyone, regardless of age or sex. If you make it a group or family project, not only can the work involved be divided among many willing hands, it will also provide opportunities for sharing and communication, which are often sadly lacking in the hustle and bustle of our hectic lives.

GETTING ORGANISED

Find your pictures The first step is to get all your photographs together.

Choose a work space If possible, find a place where there is space to lay things out. The dining-room table is ideal, especially if you can recruit friends or family members to help you.

Allocate a time slot Set aside a regular time – an afternoon or evening each week, one or two days a month or perhaps a weekend each month. Then stick to it.

Subdivide Don't focus on the whole job at once. Make a plan of what you need to do, dividing the job up into manageable sections. For example:

1 Collect all your photographs.

2 Sort them into chronological years or eras in your life – before I was married, when I worked for XYZ, after Mark was born but before Richard came along, etc. When you first start it may be slow going but you'll find your memory will become clearer as you are able to associate the pictures from one

event with those of another. This is where friends and family members might be able to help.

3 Sort the pictures of one year into the various events or occasions, starting with the most recent photographs. Put them in envelopes and write details of the event and date on the outside for easy reference.

Start your pages Don't wait to have all your photographs in chronological order before you start designing pages. The organisation is definitely the boring part, so have some fun designing pages as you go along.

Get together Include the whole family in sorting the pictures and making album pages.

START DESIGNING SOON
Once you have organised some photos into groups you can get down to the creative part of making album pages.

Taking Better Pictures

It can be very disappointing when photographs don't come up to your expectations. Here are just a few ideas to consider which may be helpful as you take photos for future memory album pages.

*P*reparation   Use a camera you feel comfortable with. There is no point in having an expensive camera which is guaranteed to take great photographs if you don't feel confident when using it. Carry fresh batteries and keep the camera loaded, ready to use. Try different brands and speeds of film so that you

Check the Background
Make sure background elements don't merge with your subject, like these flowers which appear to be growing out of his head.

Move Closer
If you have a zoom lens, zoom in on your subject, if not, move closer to ensure your subject isn't lost among all the other elements in the shot.

can find out what works best for you and your camera.

What to photograph   When taking pictures for memory album pages think in terms of the number of photographs you want to include on that page or double-page spread. Always take more photographs than you need, so you have a selection to choose from. Try to get variety, including close-ups, action shots and vertical as well as horizontal photographs. Take different views of the same scene by shooting from different angles. Learn from professional photographers who take several shots in order to get that one great photo.

Lighting   The best natural lighting generally occurs in the early morning, just after sunrise and in the late afternoon, just before sunset (see right). Of course, not everything you want to take pictures of takes place during times of optimum natural light, so consider what lighting is available. Don't shoot into the sun (with the sun behind the subject); try to use the sun as natural lighting from behind or from the side.

Background   Keep pictures simple, avoiding clutter where possible. Try to see things the way a camera does. Check the background – avoid things like tree branches that sprout from the subject's head (see above left). Look for natural frames in the foreground which can enhance and add interest. Consider including different props such as cars, homes, clothes, furniture etc. which will identify the time frame for future generations. If the background is scenery which is important, consider taking separate scenery shots. If you try to fit everything into the one shot you can end up unable to see any of it clearly because it is all so small.

Capturing the action Action shots add interest and often tell the story without words. For more natural pictures, try to take photographs while the subject is unaware of what you are doing. When taking photographs where there is lots of action, be sure you are focusing on the subject. Anticipate action by pressing the button just before it happens (see the sample below). Try a sequence of pictures in order to capture the spirit and spontaneity of the action taking place. Sometimes action shots can be posed to look spontaneous.

Focusing on the subject Try moving in close to the subjects and shooting from their level (see the example, below right). For example, when taking pictures of babies and children, get down on hands and knees. Ensure that your subjects are in the viewfinder and, if you are taking a close-up, don't cut them off at their joints. Keep the subject, not the background, in focus (see above right) otherwise you could ruin a potentially brilliant shot.

FOCUS ON THE SUBJECT
Auto-focus cameras focus on the item in the centre of the viewfinder, so make sure that this is your subject, not something in the distance.

GOOD LIGHTING
Take advantage of periods of good natural light in the early morning and evening, especially for portraits.

CAMERA, ACTION
Action shots always go down well. Follow your subject through the camera lens and try to anticipate the best moments to take your shots.

ON THEIR LEVEL
For small children and pets you'll get the best shots if you get down on their level.

THE ESSENTIALS

BEFORE YOU CAN START YOUR PAGES YOU NEED TO GET A FEW BASIC MATERIALS TOGETHER AND LEARN SOME SIMPLE SKILLS INCLUDING CROPPING, WAYS OF ARRANGING AND MOUNTING YOUR PICTURES AND JOURNALING – ADDING THE WORDS. YOU'LL FIND EVERYTHING YOU NEED TO KNOW ON THE FOLLOWING PAGES.

THE BASIC TOOL KIT

GATHERING TOGETHER MATERIALS needed to create great page layouts for your memory album should be quite simple and inexpensive. Some of the items you may already have to hand while others can be purchased fairly easily.

Photographs   Ideally don't use your original prints for your album pages, especially if you no longer have the negatives. With modern technology, you can easily make a copy from a negative or original print to use instead.

When you start out consider using colour photocopies of your photos. These can be very inexpensive if you place several pictures on a sheet of paper (using a temporary adhesive).

Paper   One of the essentials for safely preserving your photographs and page layouts is the use of acid-free and lignin-free paper. To explain it briefly, lignin causes paper to self-destruct while acid leads to deterioration. So having paper without lignin and with a neutral pH (7 or higher) is important. (Some paper suppliers use the label 'wood-free' which means lignin-free).

When purchasing paper, if it is not labelled as acid-free or lignin-free, ask the retailer to check with his supplier. While many of the papers sold in stationery and art shops are quite safe to use, some paper suppliers are not aware of the significance of labelling them as such. It is probably best to avoid recycled paper because you can never be sure what mixture of paper has been used. (More likely than not, it will include newsprint which is extremely unstable.)

Adhesives   Ensure your adhesive is photo safe and acid-free. There are many different types of suitable adhesives which can be used including white glues, glue sticks, tapes or pads and traditional photo corners. Some are instantly permanent while others allow for repositioning. It is really a case of finding the one which is best for the task at hand.

Pencils, pens and markers   A china pencil is ideal for labelling or marking photographs. The lead is very soft, so when writing on the back of photos it doesn't come through on the front, and when marking the front of a photograph it wipes off easily. There are also pens made especially for labelling. Whatever you use, take care to write without pressure so indentations don't show. Do be aware that some inks used on the back of photographs will transfer to the next photo when stacked.

Pens and markers are used for journaling and documenting as well as for decorating pages. They should be acid-free, waterproof and permanent (fade-proof). There are many different pens in various tip shapes and sizes as well as a rainbow of colours to choose from.

Album or binder   There are many different types of albums and binders on the market. Make sure the paper used is acid-free and lignin-free. If there are no page protectors you must ensure that the album itself is acid-free. (For more details see page 23.)

Page protectors   These are great. They are plastic sleeves which keep your creative work and photographs safe from moisture and heat as well as the natural oils found in human skin. Your page layouts and photographs can be enjoyed by anyone, anytime without the worry of sticky hands. Page protectors also keep everything together, where it belongs, in the event of something working itself loose over time.

Page protectors should be made of polypropylene, not vinyl. They should be of archival quality, acid-free and should not lift print or discolour your photographs. With paper and binder specifications varying between the United States and Europe, it's vital to check that your paper, binder and page protectors are compatible.

Optional extras   There are lots of extras which can be fun or helpful when producing page layouts, such as decorative pens, punches, cutters and scissors. Add any of these to supplement the basics, as and when you wish.

TOOLS OF THE TRADE
Add a few decorative options such as colourful pens, papers and punches to the basic tool kit. For instructions on making the album below see page 95.

BASIC PAGE DESIGN

YOU'RE READY TO BEGIN arranging your photographs in your album. In front of you is a blank piece of paper and around it are a pile of photographs and your basic tool kit. You're itching to have a go at arranging the pictures but a sudden panic sets in. 'How do I start to lay out my page and where do I begin?'

Memory pages are created to tell a story that can be enjoyed by family and friends today, as well as by future generations. Usually the pages are centred around photographs which illustrate special as well as ordinary events such as a wedding, day out or holiday.

There is no right or wrong way to design the pages in your album – the most important thing is that you are happy with the results. Each page reflects a bit of you, the designer, and is therefore an important part of the family memories you create.

There are some basic techniques which can help when designing creative page layouts, including cropping, matting, lettering, using templates and clip art. But before you learn about these basics, take a moment to consider the fundamentals.

ONE PAGE OR TWO?

With the exception of the very first and last pages of an album, you'll always view the album pages two at a time. These facing pages can be designed as one layout – a double-page spread – using the same theme to tell a story over two pages, or each page can be designed individually.

If you decide to design the pages individually take into account that it is more attractive and pleasing to the eye if facing pages complement each other. Try to visualise how the two pages will look together. Harmonizing them can be done quite easily by using the same colours or coordinating shades.

CHOOSING PHOTOGRAPHS

For some events you may find you have an over-abundance of great photographs while for others your supply may be very scant or of poor quality. It is essential to select the best photographs available to tell the story. However, don't be tempted to use every good photo on the subject.

Of course, it may be that you don't have any good pictures but want to record the event anyway. Choose the best and file away the rest. With a little creativity you can produce a pleasing page layout.

When making your selection of photographs, bear in mind that you will want one (or possibly two) of the best photos as the focal point of your layout. This is the feature on the page which will draw the viewer's attention. It may be the best picture you have or the photo which captures the essence of the activity or occasion.

BACKGROUND COLOUR

The right background colour can enhance your photos and layout, bringing them to life and emphasizing the theme. Choose one of the colours in the photographs or select a colour which emphasizes the mood you want to portray – bright primaries inject a sense of excitement, for example, while blue suggests a relaxed mood.

When choosing background papers, it can help to hold the focal picture over a selection of different coloured papers to find the one that appeals to you most.

CHRISTOPHER AT LUNCH

★ This colourful album page tells the story of Christopher at lunch one day on holiday in Yugoslavia.

★ The eye-catching background sets the scene. It was created by weaving coloured paper strips together to capture the pattern on the chequered tablecloth. (A paper trimmer or guillotine cuts these easily.)

★ Once the background was made we cropped and glued on the photos. The borders round the pictures were made from paper strips.

★ To ensure the text stood out, we stuck a rectangle of card, also bordered with paper strips, to the page and wrote on that. Alternatively you could write on a sticker, or even print the text from a computer.

Trimmer by Fiskars; pen from the Zig Memory System

On holiday, Yugoslavia May 1987 Christopher 9 mos.

Gold pen by Royal Sovereign

Our Christmas card for 1997 ~

Mary had a little lamb and He became our Saviour

Sarah - 4yrs., Ian - 2yrs, Hannah - 2 mos.

With a new baby in the family ~ we had all the cast of characters.

NATIVITY

★ Just one good photo and some appropriate clip art were all that was needed to tell the story on this album page.

★ The manger around the picture was made from simple strips of brown paper glued in place, while the star, angel and decorative image of the nativity scene came from the pattern library at the back of the book – clip art No. 81. We separated the angel and star and photocopied them at 150% while the nativity scene was copied at 80%. All three were cut out, coloured in with pencils and then glued in position on the album page.

BASIC TECHNIQUES

CROPPING, MATTING, DECORATING and journaling are the basic techniques you need to create decorative album pages. They can be as simple or as complex and ornate as you like.

CROPPING OUT THE BACKGROUND

The dirty old fireplace in this photo detracts from a great shot of Leanne with her favourite doll, Nellie. Cropping in close brings the focus back to the subject.

DEALING WITH GLARE

The glass-fronted frame has created an obvious glare which could ruin this photo. By cropping away that section we were able to save the special moment when this grandmother shared her love of crochet with her only granddaughter.

LIGHT CONTAMINATION

This effect can be caused by light getting into the camera or onto the film during handling or processing. However, the expression was so typical of Christopher that we wanted to use it, so we cropped out the bad part to return the focus to the subject.

CROPPING

For our purposes, cropping means the way you cut or trim photographs creatively to be used on your album page layouts. There can be any number of reasons why you might choose to crop a particular photograph.

Unattractive background If there is a lot of wasted background around the main subject of the picture or just blank space or clutter behind it you can crop it out. Likewise you may want to exclude something or someone in the background.

Bad quality If part of the photo has been overexposed but the subject matter is good or relevant to the story on your page layout you can crop out the bad sections to save the picture.

Drawing attention Cropping can be used to create interest or to focus on the subject matter, drawing attention to a special feature by using a shape that is different from the other pictures being used.

SAVING THE ORIGINALS

Before cropping, consider carefully what you will be trimming away. Does it help to put the subject into context? Does it help to date the event? Does it hold any sentimental value to you or your family? In other words, in 10 or 20 years time, will you and your family be just as interested in the old family car parked in the background as in your son playing with his toys? And isn't it fun to see old pieces of furniture, the room decor or even hairstyles and clothing that you grew up with but perhaps had forgotten after many years and several changes?

CROPPING
Cropping your pictures not only enables you to cut out unwanted or distracting areas but it also adds variety and creates attractive focal points.

We recommend that the originals of old photos or studio prints aren't cropped because of their archival value. Use a good photocopy of these for page layouts. It is best not to crop polaroid photos, so photocopy these too.

CROPPING OPTIONS

The samples on these pages show that there are many different ways to crop photographs, all of which can work well. Templates can be useful as guides and can help you visualise how the photo will look when trimmed.

Instructions for making your own templates from the patterns at the back of the book can be found on page 31. Drinking glasses or bowls are great for making circles, while biscuit cutters can be used for novelty shapes.

MATTING

Whether you crop your pictures or not, a way to emphasize photos is to mount them on paper, a technique called matting. By using paper to create a frame around the photograph, you can enhance it. Use two or more co-ordinated papers to add more variety.

It is quite easy to matt a photograph. Once you have cropped the picture to the desired shape and size, glue it to the chosen paper and trim around it, leaving an equal amount of paper on all sides. A paper trimmer is an invaluable tool if you do quite a lot of matting (see pages 26-27).

FIRST DAY AT SCHOOL
(below)
These pictures all have double matts to enliven the page. The yellow inner matts add a bright, fresh touch while the grey ones pick up on the colour of the uniform and background paper.

Pens from the Zig Memory System

CHRISTOPHER'S
CHRISTENING
(right)
A decorative
frame can give a
picture greater
weight in your
album. This one is
photocopied from
page 100 onto
lightly tinted
paper and then
coloured with felt-
tip pens. (See
page 86 for
further details on
recreating this
layout.)

GODPARENTS
Here's an example
of how you can
use the templates
in this book. This
layout was easy to
create by photo-
copying the hearts
template from
page 106 onto
blue paper and
colouring it
in.(See page 87
for further details
on recreating this
layout.)

DECORATING

There are many forms of embellishment which can help to create attractive page layouts. Creating frames or
borders around photographs or pages
can be as simple or as detailed as you
wish. These can be made from paper
(as in matting or a template) or created using pens and markers (page 28)
and a few basic shapes. Die cuts or
simple shapes cut from paper (page
30) that go with the chosen theme
are easy to use and very inexpensive.

Clip-art motifs which can be
photocopied onto the page layout and then coloured in are
also a popular way of creating a
theme. (There are lots of these
for you to use on pages 110-
121). Alternatively, use the templates
on pages 100-108. While these techniques are covered in more detail in
Creative Options (page 30) it is worth
knowing about them early on
because they are so
easy to use.

Christopher's Christening
9 May 1987
St Albans, Hertfordshire

USING PAGE TEMPLATES

*   Make a photocopy of the chosen
image from pages 100-108 onto plain
white paper.
*   Plan your page – where the photos
will go, what colour background you
want, and so on.
*   Take the photocopy of the template
page and photocopy that onto your
chosen background paper (of course,
if you want a white background you
can skip this step and use the copy
on white paper). If the template
page is not the exact size of your
album or binder, it can be
reduced or enlarged on the photocopier. For larger square
albums, the finished template
page can be mounted or even
framed and mounted onto
the larger page.
*   Mount your pictures,
decorate the pages (colour
in) and add whatever text
you wish.

JOURNALING

Memory albums can be so much more than just a presentation of your life in photographs. With just a little effort you can transform them into interesting story books that can be enjoyed today and for many years to come.

Too many of us have come across old-fashioned black-and-white photographs of people we don't recognise. How sad when we discover that there is no one left to enlighten us on who these people are, when the photographs were taken and if or how we are connected.

By adding the answers to the basic questions of good journalism: Who? What? When? Where? and Why? we can add information which will prove invaluable when our memories grow dimmer and future generations want to know more about their ancestors.

Journaling is great fun. In addition to the basic questions listed above, there are other things you can add that will be enjoyed by the viewer, such as an associated story, a favourite expression or sentimental memory.

With today's technology it is easy to use various fancy fonts for the journaling of your pages. Don't be tempted to use these all the time, however. Handwritten journaling has a great deal of sentimental value.

PRINT OR WRITE
These two examples of journaling (below left and right) include one version which was was hand-written and another which was printed from a computer. One may be neater, but the other is more personal. (See page 83 for details on recreating this Halloween page.)

Paper by Hot Off the Press; stamp design © 1997 Stampendous Inc. Rubber Stamps

DOG GONE
(above)
By putting the pictures at the top and bottom of this page we left plenty of space in the middle for journaling. We simply hand wrote the text between the diagonal lines of paw prints on the paper. The bone is clip art No. 46.

USING JUST THE ESSENTIALS

LET THE PAGES in this section and beyond inspire you to create eye-catching memory album pages using just the tools and techniques covered so far with a few of your favourite additions, such as decorative papers and clip art.

As you look at the page layouts throughout this book you'll notice that most use the basic techniques covered on the previous pages with a few embellishments and extras added for variety or ease. It is simple to give photos, good and bad, a lift by cropping them or placing them over a matt. Try using templates and clip art too. These provide an inexpensive way to decorate pages, so to start you off you can use the selection at the back of this book (see page 110).

These samples show what can be done using just the essentials covered so far. With the most basic materials and equipment (some of which you probably have already) you will soon see just how easy it is to create your own memory page layouts. But be warned, it is extremely addictive.

BOXING CHAMPS
You can make attractive layouts very simply. Here we cropped the photographs and used a contrasting paper for the single matts, bold heading and journaling box.(See page 60 for details on recreating this page.)

BJ THE CAT
Contrasting colour matts frame the photos of this inquisitive little creature. A form of doodling using different pen tips can create borders as well as tell a story. (See page 68 for details on recreating this page.)

PUTTING IT ALL TOGETHER

ALTHOUGH IT'S EASY putting page layouts, protector sheets, binders or albums together, it is important to take your time deciding which type of album you want to use, for what types or themes of pages and why to ensure everything pulls together.

RING BINDERS

A ring binder is a very popular format because it allows such easy access to your memory pages. For this reason it is the format we have chosen to show you throughout this book. The page layouts are slipped into clear page protectors then put into the binder.

The pages can be turned easily and are protected from sticky or dirty hands, as well as the natural oils in human skin which may damage your pages and photos. Pages can be added or removed as and when you like, without spoiling the collection.

There are some very nice binder covers available which look very smart if the binders are to be on display. There are also ways in which you can use your creative talents to make or decorate your own album (see pages 92-95).

When choosing a binder, it is best to opt for one that has a D-ring so that your pages lie flat when the binder is closed. Selecting one which is a little larger than the standard size will protect the page edges.

EXPANDABLE ALBUMS

Expandable albums allow the addition of pages within the binding, giving you some of the versatility of a binder with the elegance of the spiral-bound album. The pages lie flat and close, a plus for creating double-page spreads without a gap between pages.

SPIRAL-BOUND ALBUMS

These albums have a more sophisticated look and are easy to use. They are available in a wide choice of sizes. The pages lie flat and fit close together when open which is particularly good for double-page spreads. When choosing an album of this type, it is essential to ensure that it is acid-free.

Unlike binders or expandable albums, pages cannot be added to these albums. Sheet protectors are not available, so one needs to be careful how the album is handled. Generally the pages of a spiral-bound album come in just one colour so to change the background you must glue on another sheet of paper.

BINDER OPTIONS

A spiral-bound album looks wonderful but it can be quite limiting as pages cannot be added. Both expandable albums and ring binders do allow for the addition of pages.

CREATIVE OPTIONS

THERE ARE MANY WAYS OF ADDING CREATIVE DETAIL TO YOUR PAGES, WHATEVER YOUR LEVEL OF ARTISTIC TALENT. DECORATIVE PAPERS, CUTTERS AND PUNCHES, PENS AND MARKERS, TEMPLATES AND STENCILS ARE JUST SOME OF THE TOOLS YOU CAN USE.

DECORATIVE PAPERS

BACKGROUND PAPERS can add huge decorative appeal to your pages, emphasize a theme or bring out a colour. What's more, they are fun to choose and to use.

SWIMMING LESSONS
For this page we found the perfect commercial paper to fit the theme and enhance the photographs (see page 54).

More and more commercially printed decorative papers are coming onto the market. Many are acid-free which means they are perfect to use for your album pages. There are hundreds of colours and designs to fit every conceivable occasion or theme.

If you can't find just the right background paper, you can easily make your own. Everyone is using paint effects to decorate furniture or the walls in their homes, so why not use similar techniques to decorate background paper for your memory album pages?

Colourwashing Background Paper

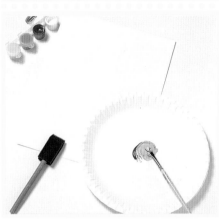

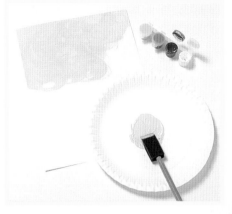

1 Dampen a brush and remove as much water as possible (we used a sponge brush). On a paper plate mix a little colour – here blue and white acid-free paint from Cherished Memories by Delta. (Adding a few small drops of black will give a greyer colour if you like.)

2 Using swirling, scrubbing motions paint the paper as desired. Leave some of the page unpainted or fill in the entire page, as we did.

DECORATIVE PAPERS
If you don't want to decorate your own paper, choose one of the many acid-free and lignin-free papers on the market. (See the Suppliers, page 124 for a list of useful contacts and suppliers.)

3 Once dry add dots with a pen. We chose a silver marker by Royal Sovereign but white would also be nice. (See Winter Fun, page 76 for a design using the finished paper.)

DECORATIVE CUTTING TOOLS

DECORATIVE-EDGE SCISSORS, punches, corner edgers, circle cutters, trimmers and guillotines all make it easy to create attractive effects in no time. Experiment with some of these tools on scrap paper to find out just what exciting effects you can produce.

Decorative-edge scissors These are great for giving a fancy edge to photos and mats and for making creative borders. There are many different finishes to choose from including zigzag, wave, scallop and deckle.

Punches These enable you to punch out a variety of small shapes which can be used to add creative flare to your album pages. There are so many different punch designs available, it would be hard to mention them all. Some of the more popular ones include hearts, stars, moons, cats, dogs, flowers and teddy bears.

Corner edgers Similar to punches, these are used specifically for cutting the corners of photos, matts or background papers. They range from a punch which simply rounds off corners to more elaborate punches which produce fancy designs.

Circle cutters These useful tools can cut perfect circles of different sizes quickly and with little fuss. There are various types on the market, but they all operate in basically the same way. These are very useful for the dedicated memory page designer.

Guillotines and trimmers If you want to cut straight edges quickly and efficiently, invest in one of these. With a trimmer or guillotine you can get a truly straight edge which is not easily obtained when cutting by hand with scissors.

NOTE
If you have any difficulty obtaining the cutting tools or any of the other products mentioned in this book, refer to the Supplier's list on pages 124-127.

CUTTING TOOLS
Decorative-edge scissors create attractive edges in no time, but you'll also want to try out punches (right) and corner edgers (top right).

Using Cutting Tools

Corner edger Use this simple tool to punch out the corners of a photo or its matts. With some punches, like this one, you are left with small punched motifs which you can also use on your pages.

Circle cutter Slide your photograph or paper under this lightweight cutter to cut perfect circles in seconds. To adjust the size of the circle simply loosen the knob in the centre and slide the cutting arm.

Trimmer and guillotine A trimmer, (left) has a concealed blade which you run along a ruler edge to trim the paper. A guillotine (right) has a cutting blade which chops down on paper or card to create a clean cut. A trimmer is much safer than a guillotine but may not be able to cut through very thick card.

JOE LOVES CONTAINERS
A corner edger and punch give a decorative finish to the picture of Joe in the red bucket plus its matts. (See page 76 for further details and the full page layout.)

PENS, PENCILS & MARKERS

THERE ARE ALL SORTS of pens and markers available with a multitude of tips that come in an unbelievable range of colours. They can be used to create different effects for lettering in captions, headings or journaling. They can also be used to embellish pages and to create decorative paper as in our samples.

With all the great pens and markers available, the possibilities for creating decorative details on your pages are endless. Something as simple as combining various straight lines (drawn with the help of a ruler) in different colours can create a quite dramatic effect, as shown below.

Often the photograph or artwork you plan to use on your page can provide you with the inspiration for creating decorative backgrounds. On the Autographs page (below) we made our own plaid design using a ruler and a wide-tip pen and added swirls with a fine-tip pen. On Megan (page 53) we used a variety of pen tips to achieve an attractive design of coil roses, wavy stripes and pin-dot clusters.

JOURNALING

Pens and markers are also important for headings, captions and journaling. Many people don't journal because they don't feel confident about their handwriting and are afraid that they will mess up their pages if they try to write things in their own hand. If you would like to improve your handwriting or want ideas on ways to vary handwriting, here are a few hints and tips.

AUTOGRAPHS
Enliven plain background pages with acid-free pens, as here, where pens in two colours were used to create the bright plaid. (See page 72 for further details.)

Draw a very faint pencil line as a guide to help your writing stay straight. Draw a second parallel line if you have difficulty making letters of equal size.

Practice, practice and practice. There are times when we have to wait for one thing or another – for children to come out of school, at the dentist, at the airport, etc. Keep a note pad and pen in your bag and practice your lettering whenever there is an odd ten minutes or so. Apart from improving your handwriting, it will help pass the time profitably.

Begin by printing (with separate letters) rather than writing in script (with joined-up letters).

Start by just drawing straight, even lines, then move on to writing the alphabet with all the letters straight up and down. In the beginning, avoid slanting letters. Look critically at your letters and compare them to the samples we have included. Take note of what you like and what you don't.

Next practice making nice rounded circles, half circles and three-quarter circles. Now practice letters which include circles – b, c, d, e, g, o, p, etc.

Practice writing letters close together. Try to get the spacing between letters equal. Next practice writing words and titles in a specific space, thus learning how to judge the size of lettering you can afford to use for a given area of the page.

Develop your own style. Observe other forms of lettering and when you see something you really like, find ways of including it in your style.

Once you have developed your style of printing, experiment with different ways of embellishing it to make it interesting for different pages and themes.

PEN POWER

These colourful pens are acid-free, so you can use them as much as you like without fear of damaging your photos. They come in some wonderful colours and both thick and thin nibs. For the alphabets see pages 122-123.

TEMPLATES, STENCILS, FANCY RULERS & DIE-CUT SHAPES

THERE ARE MANY TOOLS available today which are great for adding just the right touch to your page design. They can also make the tedious jobs go more quickly, leaving you more time for the fun parts. Templates, stencils, fancy rulers and die-cut shapes are covered here, but keep your eyes open for new gadgets that are always coming along.

Templates The templates that we are talking about here are sheets of plastic or clear acrylic which have various shapes punched or cut out, like stencils. The variety of shapes is endless. There are ovals, circles, squares, octagons, triangles, stars, hearts and many more which work well with cropping photographs. Also available are templates with novelty shapes such as animals, ice-cream cones, clouds, crayons, trophies, angels, etc.

With time and patience you can make a template of each of your favourite shapes (see right). We suggest using the acrylic sheets available for use with overhead projectors.

Stencils Stencilling is a popular hobby and the technique is quite easy to use for creating decorative album pages. There are stencils especially made for memory page layouts, including some designed for page borders, fancy corners, frames and headings. These come in a wide variety of decorative themes.

Fancy rulers There is a large selection of decorative rulers on the market and more are being added all the time. The decorative edge can be used to draw attractive borders, page corners or frames. The design could even be cut out, giving the same sort of look as decorative-edge scissors.

Die-cut shapes These basic shapes made of coloured paper are called die cuts after the commercial machine that was traditionally used to make them. They can be found in craft, stationery and educational supply shops. The choice of shapes is huge and more are being added all the time.

Die cuts provide a quick and easy way to embellish your page. Because of the simplicity of their design, they are easy to make (see right).

RULERS AND TEMPLATES
Decorative-edge rulers and templates like these make quick work of adding neat embellishments to your pages.

Making Templates

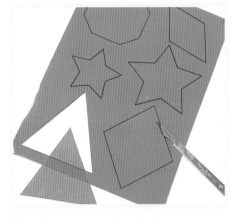

1   Trace the shapes you want to use onto paper, leaving adequate space between them.

2   Place a sheet of acrylic (the type used with overhead projectors) over the pattern. Cut out the shapes.

JAM SESSION
Decorative rulers helped to create the gold embossed borders down the left side this page. The darker coloured paper behind allows the fancy edges to show up more clearly. (See page 77 for further details.)

3   Your template is ready to use to crop photographs or make die-cut shapes.

We were visiting Grandma and Grand for Christmas. The children were so excite show them what they had learned in their lessons. They were so surprised when G dug out his saxophone from college and joined in!

RUBBER STAMPS

RUBBER STAMPING is a fun technique that can be enjoyed by adults and children of all abilities and is sure to give great results with minimal practice and time.

Rubber stamping has become such a phenomenon that you can find rubber stamps on virtually every conceivable subject or theme. The styles of different artists are also reflected in the wide choice of stamps available so you are bound to find just what you need.

Stamps can be used to create borders, decorative corners, frames around pictures or journaling, decorative embellishments and so much more.

There are various techniques of using stamps. You can stamp with pigment inks in a variety of colours as we have done on Special Friends (below right). Alternatively, the stamped images can be made more colourful by using pencils or markers to fill in the blank spaces, as in Christopher in the Garden (below). For a different look, try embossing powders which create a raised image as in Jam Session (pages 31 and 77).

While there are thousands of rubber stamps in detailed designs available in the shops today, we thought it might be fun to make our own tiny stamps to make decorative paper (see opposite).

CHRISTOPHER IN THE GARDEN
Here the stamping was done with black ink and then coloured in with markers. (See page 52 for details on creating this layout.)

Stamp designs © 1997 Stampendous Inc. Rubber Stamps and © 1997 Precious Moments Inc. licensee Stampendous Inc. Stamp usage limited to personal non-commercial purposes

Making a Mini Stamp

1   Take some inexpensive pencils with erasers on one end. Mark out a simple pattern on each one such as a square, zigzag or triangle.

2   Carefully use a small craft knife to cut away the part of the eraser not needed for your design.

SPECIAL FRIENDS
Here we used inks
in several colours
to stamp the
pencil-top shapes
and the creatures
which emphasize
the outdoor theme
of this page. (See
page 65 for details
of this layout.)

3   Ink the end of the rubber and stamp it on paper to try out the effect.

Stamp designs © 1997 Stampendous Inc. Rubber Stamps

CLIP ART & COMPUTER SOFTWARE

WHILE THE CONCEPT of clip art isn't new, with the accessibility and cost-effectiveness of photocopies today, it is becoming a popular way of adding artistic decoration to various forms of paper crafts. It lends itself perfectly to the creation of memory album pages.

Clip art is artwork or line drawings which can be cut out and used in a number of ways. On many of the page layouts shown in this book it was used to highlight and embellish. You'll find quite an extensive collection of clip art covering a wide range of themes and occasions on pages 112-121.

Background paper by Hot Off the Press; corner rounder by Marvy Uchida; regal corner edger by Fiskars; pencils by Derwent.

A little kiss in the moonlight!

RAWHIDE
WESTERN TOWN & STEAKHOUSE
Scottsdale, Arizona

PICTURE YOURSELF IN THE OLD WEST.

Kathy's in trouble again!

WANTED DEAD OR ALIVE
The Vampin' Stampin' Gang
Marion Wright, Carol Nelson, Dean Collins, Janice Slowey and Kathy Sanders

The Achey Breaky Dancers Anne and Sean Flynn

Shall we ever forget the night this mild mannered group from England, hit the little western town of Rawhide? We were nearly rolling on the floor laughing as they dressed for their souvenir photo. What a sport our new friend Dean turned out to be. Rawhide shall never be the same.

An end of the evening photo of our whole group!
June 12, 1993

RAWHIDE
With this double-page spread we used the badge, boots and hat, clip art Nos 34, 37 and 38, to emphasize the western theme. The poster was a brochure – we replaced their photo with ours. Buffer the brochure to prevent contact with the photos.

Using Clip Art

1   Photocopy the artwork from the back of the book onto white paper. Cut out the chosen design, leaving a margin of about 3-6mm (⅛-¼in) around the outer edge.

2   Lay out your photographs on your background paper (A) and determine the position of the clip art. Make a photocopy guide (B) by placing the clip art in position on a blank piece of white paper.

3   Take the photocopy guide and photo-copy it onto the background paper. Now position your photographs. You can colour in the clip art if you wish. Alternatively, clip art can be cut out in detail, coloured in and then glued in position.

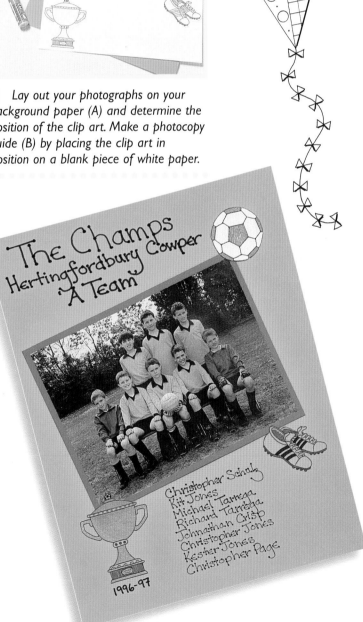

MEMORABILIA – KEEPER ENVELOPE

As you collate pictures to tell the story of a particular occasion, you can add other items relating to the event. Tickets, invitations, locks of hair, newspaper clippings, greetings cards and a host of other small items can all be used to bring life to a page, and using them in your album is also a good way of saving such precious memorabilia.

Due to the high acid content of items like newsprint and to the unknown acidity of other printed items, memorabilia should be carefully preserved in order to protect your photographs from acid migration. Through physical contact or acidic vapours, the area touched by an acidic item can change colour and your photographs could be sullied.

Special de-acidifying aerosols are available but they can be quite pricey. Luckily there are other ways of protecting against acidity. In the case of newsprint, for example, you can make a

colour photocopy which will preserve the documentation and at the same time provide an authentic look. Alternatively, look out for special transparent envelopes which come in a variety of sizes and can be used for sealing memorabilia while still enabling you to view them. These envelopes can be mounted on the page.

If you like the idea of using a transparent envelope you can easily make your own following the instructions opposite. Use clear plastic or cellophane so you can see the item inside.

50TH WEDDING ANNIVERSARY
The gold bow indicates the keeper envelope on this page which holds treasured confetti. The envelope has been attached with the folds face down to display an anniversary greeting. (See page 86 for details on recreating this page layout.)

Making a Keeper Envelope

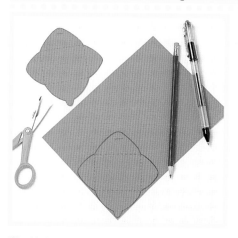

1 Make a card template by photocopying the pattern on page 111. Cut out the photocopied pattern and trace it onto stiff card. Cut out the card to use as your template. Place the template over a piece of clear plastic or cellophane and cut around it using scissors or a craft knife on a cutting mat.

3 Your memorabilia item can be placed on either side of the coloured card depending on how you wish to mount the envelope on the page. The folded sides can be mounted to face up, as shown right or placed at the back and glued to the page (see the 50th wedding anniversary celebration, left).

2 Cut a piece of card to fit inside the fold lines (indicated on the pattern with broken lines). This gives the envelope stability and provides a backing for the item to go inside. Place the card and your chosen item on the plastic or cellophane, then fold up the sides along the fold lines and secure with a sticker or dab of glue.

LEANNE'S FIRST HAIRCUT
A lock of hair is just the sort of thing you might want to preserve in a keeper envelope. The folded sides are arranged face up so you can remove the lock of hair if you wish. (See page 53 for details on recreating this page layout.)

POCKET PAGE

AN ALTERNATIVE TO a keeper envelope for storing memorabilia such as cards, programmes, awards and similar items is a pocket page. This is a great way of keeping everything relevant to a particular event together.

Whereas a keeper envelope secures an item permanently, with a pocket page the pocket is kept open so you can remove the item(s) inside. To make a pocket page you will need two pieces of acid-free paper and adhesive.

CHRISTMAS FIREPLACE
Paper was cut into a brick pattern to create this pocket which makes it look like part of the fireplace the girls are sitting on. We used the pocket to store Christmas cards from special loved ones. (See page 85 for further details.)

Making a Pocket Page

1   Take a sheet of acid-free paper and cut it to the size of the pocket. The items to be placed inside will determine how large the pocket needs to be.

2   Position and glue the pocket to the album page with acid-free adhesive. Keep the top of the pocket open for access by gluing around the bottom and sides only.

HEIDI'S CHRISTENING
Here the pocket portion of the page was turned at an angle to create a feature for storing special mementoes. (See page 86 for details on creating this layout.)

3   Decorate your page and fill the pocket with your chosen item(s) of memorabilia.

Certificate of Baptism
Heidi Lyn Ekema
is Christened this day
April 25, 1982

at the Epis

STICKERS

NOT ONLY DO STICKERS provide one of the easiest ways of decorating pages, they are also a lot of fun. The right sticker can emphasize the chosen theme, draw attention to the particular characteristics of the subject and fill in unwanted blank space. And what could be easier – just peel off the backing paper and press into position.

Like rubber stamps and clip art, stickers come in a multitude of different artistic styles and cover every imaginable theme and occasion. There are stickers that can be used for borders, decorative corner stickers and alphabet stickers that can be used for headlines and captions as well as animals, insects, birds, babies, children, adults, household items and even sports

50s stickers by the American Sticker Company; Western
Stickers by Mrs Grossman's ™

Stickers by Stickopotamus Inc.™

DRESSING UP
Here stickers helped us unite pictures from entirely different occasions placed on different background papers. We covered the diagonal dividing line between the papers with sticker strips cut in half.

SARAH IN THE BATH
Bath-time stickers emphasized the theme here and helped to fill in blank space.
(See page 49 for more details.)

equipment. You name it, there is probably at least a handful of stickers available on the subject. In fact, stickers are becoming very collectible items in their own right.

When using stickers to embellish memory album pages, ensure they don't cause long-term damage to your album pages and photographs by checking that they are made from acid-free paper and use acid-free adhesive.

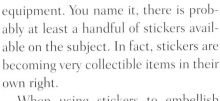

Bryce and Madeline stickers from Melissa Neufeld, Inc. © Jone Hallmark. Available in the UK from First Class Stamps Ltd. Tel: 01328 851 449

Wave, seagull, scallop scissors and wave blade by Fiskars, corner rounder by Marvy Uchida; alphabet stickers by Frances Meyer Inc.™; birthday stickers by Stickopotomus Inc.™

BEN'S BIRTHDAY PAGE
Colourful stickers express the fun and excitement of this celebration. Bold double matts trimmed with decorative-edge scissors complete the look.

Creating themed

CONTENTS

album pages...

Bryce and Madelaine stickers from Melissa Neufeld Inc. © Jone Hallmark. Available from First Class Stamps Ltd.

QUICK LAYOUTS

WITH MOST PEOPLE'S TIME AT A PREMIUM THESE DAYS, WE
FELT IT WAS IMPORTANT TO SHOW THAT CREATING ATTRACTIVE ALBUM PAGES NEEDN'T TAKE
FOREVER. HERE ARE A FEW EXAMPLES OF LAYOUTS YOU COULD RECREATE IN JUST TWENTY
MINUTES OR SO. LET THEM INSPIRE YOU TO CREATE YOUR OWN VERSIONS.

Most of the layouts in this book can
be completed in less than an hour, but
the wide range of layouts on this spread
show what is possible when time is
particularly tight.

Paper by Hot Off the Press; pen from the Zig Memory System

ALY

★ *This background paper was so
striking that we had to use it, and
these photos of little Aly playing
with rose petals seemed to go
perfectly with it.*
★ *Because the paper was so ornate
there was no need for any additional
decoration.*

Pens from the Zig Memory System and by Royal Sovereign; Mono Adhesive by Tombow

FOOTBALL CHAMPS

★ *This layout uses the trophy (No.
39), football (No. 40) and boots
(No. 41) from the clip art section to
give it a lively touch. (See page 35
for details on using clip art.) To slip
the photo into place we used a craft
knife to cut around the edges of the
trophy and boots.* ★ *We chose a
bright orange backing paper to complement the players' shirts and a
bright green paper for the matt to
complement the two goalies' shirts.*

SAN DIEGO

★ This smart background paper picks up on the pattern of the turtle's shell rather nicely. To make sure it co-ordinates totally, we added cream matts under the pictures and used the same colour for the title.

PRETTY IN PINK

★ This is a good way of using up scraps of paper, and it's quick to do. Just layer rectangles and strips of paper, decorate them with pens or stamps and add your photo.

ANIMAL PARK

★ Placing one background sheet over another at an angle is a quick way of giving a page a new look – just trim off the upper paper where it extends beyond the base paper.
★ Here we highlighted the pictures with simple yellow matts and added some animal stickers to emphasize the safari feel.

BABY

EVERYONE LOVES A BABY, AND PHOTOGRAPHING THEM AND THEIR EARLY DEVELOPMENT IS A POPULAR PASTIME FOR PARENTS AND GRANDPARENTS ALIKE. AND WHY NOT? MAKING PAGES FROM THESE EARLY DAYS CAN BE A LOT OF FUN AND THEY WILL BE ENJOYED FOR YEARS AND YEARS.

Everyone has their own ideas about what it's important to record in a baby's growth and development, but here are some suggestions to help you start thinking along the right lines.

• **Start early** Begin keeping records even before the baby is born. Data such as the positive results of the pregnancy test or ultra-sound scan photos could be of interest in years to come.

• **Keep important memorabilia** Hold onto the birth announcements, hospital notes, a copy of the birth certificate, cards and anything else relating to the baby and its birth. These can be mounted on pages in keeper envelopes (see pages 36-37) or kept in pocket pages (see pages 38-39).

• **Feelings** If you like, write a letter to the unborn child telling him or her about your feelings of anticipation, hopes for the future, plans, or even about how the pregnancy is progressing. Do the same right after your child is born, giving details of the events preceding and during the birth. Include the names of medical staff who cared for you and your baby. Start a journal of your new routine. Keep records of gifts and flowers as well as visitors. Most of all, write down your baby's particular characteristics.

• **Firsts** Take pictures and jot down details of all the 'firsts' – the first feed, the first bath and the first ride in the car. Don't forget the first smile, the first laugh, the first time he or she crawls, sits up, stands, walks, runs, etc. Plan for these ahead by having the camera ready and loaded with film.

• **Background information** Create a page which includes information on what was happening in the world at the time of birth. Include newspaper clippings of important events, both local and global. You may wish to add basic data such as the cost of staple food items, the cost of the pram or a baby outfit, for comparisons in later years.

• **Progress report** Record your baby's progress on a regular basis. By taking a photograph in the same place (such as daddy's arms or a favourite chair) on the same day every month you will be able to monitor growth and development visually.

BABY LEANNE

★ *It's a lovely idea to include thoughts you had at the very early stages of your child's development. For Leanne there will now always be a record of how she got her name.*

★ *To keep those precious cards of congratulation from friends and relatives, this page has a pocket (see page 38) made by cutting the top sheet at an angle. The blocks which spell out Leanne's name are copies of clip art No. 5 photocopied onto lavender paper; the letters are stickers. If you prefer, you could print letters from a computer and glue them on.*

THINKING OF YOU

LEANNE

May 10
1981

Leanne-
You were such a tiny
little thing when you were
born. The name we had
selected just seemed too
big for you, so Daddy
suggested "Leanne"
and I loved it!

Paper by Hot Off the Press; scallop scissors by Fiskars; heart punch by Marvy Uchida; pencils by Derwent

Christopher Brian
Born- Sunday 12:38 am
August 3, 1986
7 lbs. 4 oz.

"You know mummy,
I think everything here
is going to be okay!"

IT'S A BOY!

★ This page features a clever way of including intimate details about the baby – hidden inside the fold-out nappy (see inset far left) are baby Christopher's vital statistics. You can copy this idea by using the nappy pattern on page 111 and attach a paper heart, or even a nappy pin to the front.

★ Decorate your page with clip art, as here. The bear is a photocopy of clip art No. 9 which has been coloured in. The heart used for the text is a basic shape from page 110 cut out with decorative-edge scissors. The tiny hearts are punched out of contrasting paper and glued on.

Paper and stickers by NRN Designs

BABY AARON

★ Here's one way of saving important memorabilia like the birth certificate or birth details and things which are a bit of fun, like your baby's footprints or hand prints. Highlight them with some colourful matts, like the double blue and yellow ones here (see page 19). You can also use the matts to add creative shapes, like the stunning triple star matts (see Basic Shapes page 110) around the baby's portrait.

★ This is also the place for any favourite lines of poetry or suitable sayings. Here we added a poem on a cloud, clip art No. 15, to tie in with the star. These are set off by the star-spangled background paper and charming baby stickers.

CHRISTOPHER'S FIRST BIRTHDAY

★ *Make a birthday page really special. This one is like a present itself, with a big bow and greetings card.*

★ *The bow is clip art No. 6 copied onto yellow paper, and the '1st birthday' is clip art No. 7. (We cut the number away from the rest of the artwork so it would fit in with our page layout.) We cut the ribbon from matching card using decorative-edge scissors.*

★ *The card is a 6 x 10cm (2½ x 4in) rectangle of paper folded in half, bordered with a marker and cut with decorative-edge scissors.*

Paper by Provo Craft; stamp designs © 1997 Stampendous Inc. Rubber Stamps; mini scallop scissors by Fiskars

With the distance between us, we don't get to see each other as much as we would like. What fun we had celebrating Christopher's birthday together at Grandma and Grandpa's house. Mummy and Daddy, Uncle Don and Auntie Debbie and of course Aaron and Keanan. They loved showing him what this birthday business was all about.

Happy Birthday Christopher

Paper by Hot Off the Press; scallop scissors by Fiskars; corner rounder by Marvey Uchida; stickers by Stickopotomus Inc. ™

SARAH IN THE BATH

★ *Everyday events, like bathtime, are fun to look back on, particularly if it is a 'first', such as the first time in an adult bath or with a new toy.*

★ *Choose suitable papers for the background and matts, then position your photographs. Once you are happy with the arrangement, add the words and finally fill in the spaces with stickers or relevant clip art, such as the bubbles (No. 2).*

★ *To see this layout full-size, refer to page 40.*

THE EARLY YEARS

KEEPING A RECORD OF OUR LITTLE ONES AS THEY GROW UP IS A WAY OF PRESERVING THE VARIOUS STAGES OF THEIR DEVELOPMENT. THE TIME YOU INVEST IN CAPTURING THE ESSENCE OF THEIR PERSONALITIES AND CHARACTERS IN PHOTOGRAPHS AND TEXT WILL PROVIDE YOU — AND THEM — WITH REMINDERS OF THOSE PRECIOUS YEARS.

One of the most wonderful things about your children's early years is that you can begin to include them in the active side of preserving memories. Together you can build a relationship based on having fun together, sharing and communicating. Here are some ideas for recording this time and ways of including your children.

• **Words and actions** Whenever you can, jot down your children's memorable words and actions. As time goes by many will be lost forever if not recorded somewhere.

• **Art and writing** Include some of your children's drawings or paintings and samples of their writing within the pages of your memory album.

• **Friends and playmates** Keep a journal, supported with photographs, of important friends and playmates.

• **Likes and dislikes** Make a list of your children's likes and dislikes. Include such things as their favourite colour, career choice, favourite television programme and character, etc.

• **Global events** Include details of important events in the world around you to set the scene.

• **Prizes and certificates** Include awards, school projects, certificates or anything which will help to tell the story of your children's development.

• **Personal involvement** Get your children involved in text. If they are too young to write themselves use an interview technique.

• **Their own albums** Let your children start albums of their own. Let them have spare photos or colour photocopies of their favourite photographs.

CHRISTOPHER ON HIS TRAIN

★ *This layout shows how you can use several photos from one session to capture your child in action, give movement to the page and make your album more lively and exciting. Christopher adored his Thomas the Tank Engine, so we wanted to give full weight to it on the page.*

★ *Notice that we carefully cut out the photos of Christopher on his engine in silhouette. This enabled us to do more with the pictures, to remove the distracting background details and to ensure continuity on the page. We hand drew the tracks linking the pictures.*

★ *Finally, notice the station house. This was created by taking two photocopies of the building, clip art No. 48 at the back of the book. We cut open the doors on one copy and stuck just the doors from the other copy inside them. That way the doors look equally good whether closed (detail above) or left open (right). We put pictures of Christopher's cousins inside the doors.*

all aboard

Hertford North Train Station

Train Tickets Sold Here

CHRISTOPHER- These pictures were taken when you were about two years old. This toy was your favourite because you loved the video about "Thomas the Tank". You used to love to rush about and you could really move with this train on wheels, but most of all you loved it when somebody would push you.

Paper by Provo Craft; stickers by Melissa Neufeld; mounting tape by Therm O Web

Pen by Royal Sovereign; stamp designs © 1997 Stampendous Inc. Rubber Stamps and © 1997 Precious Moments Inc. licensee Stampendous Inc. Stamp usage limited to personal non-commercial purposes; scissors by Fiskars; corner rounder by Marvy Uchida

BATHTIME BUDDIES

★ Bathtime can be a great source of photos for your album. Notice the progression of the photos across this spread, with Hannah starting off almost hidden inside the bath and clambering out at the end. This type of progression helps to tell the story and keeps the viewer's attention.

★ A few stickers complete the effect.

CHRISTOPHER IN THE GARDEN

★ Decorative stamps and scissors provide simple ways of enlivening your page layouts. Here we used stamps to create the small checked frame and add the printed image.

★ The checks were stamped onto plain paper and then coloured in.

★ We cropped the photo with decorative-edge scissors and trimmed the squares with a corner rounder.

Pens from the Zig Memory System; seagull scissors by Fiskars; pencils by Derwent

a big orange Halloween pumpkin that she had full of *all sorts of tiny treasures. She insisted that at take some home with me and*

Megan

Such a funny little girl she was that day! Spring time and she's toting around

LEANNE'S FIRST HAIRCUT
(below)

★ A child's first proper haircut can be a momentous event.

★ We kept a lock of hair in a keeper envelope (see page 37) which we cut from the clear plastic of a page protector and attached with ribbon through punched holes. The scissors are clip art No. 21 coloured in with acid-free markers.

★ The compact was made by drawing two circles about 6mm (¼in) apart, which we cut out to leave a small hinge of paper. We cut a second double circle shape and cut out the centres to leave a border of about 1cm (½in). We glued silver paper behind one opening and the photo behind the other, then stuck the two double circle shapes together and decorated the outside.

You used to go to the beauty shop with Mommy

and Grandma. You felt so grown up when it was finally

August 13, 1983 age 2

Paper by HyGloss; pen from Royal Sovereign; make-up stickers by Stickopotamus Inc. ™

your turn. The manicurist even polished your

nails. Grandma gave you her compact so you could... your first haircut.

MEGAN *(above)*

★ We made this decorative background paper ourselves, drawing wavy lines and adding small, tight coils for roses and teardrops for leaves. We also drew the clusters of dots by hand with a fine-tip pen.

★ The bird is clip art No. 49 and the birdhouse is No. 50, copied onto white paper and coloured in. We cut the grass at the bottom of the birdhouse pole from part of a photo of real grass we had cropped off.

★ When text goes around an edge, like this, it's a good idea to practise on scrap paper to check the fit.

Paper © Hot Off the Press

On Holiday to Croatia - 1987

Mummy and Daddy took you, Mark, and Richard to Porec, Croatia. You were only nine months old. We visited with Grandpa Schulz, Aunty Misha, Aunty Seka and cousins Inez, Dolibor and Zoran. We stayed at the Hotel Parentium, which was located on it's own peninsula.

You didn't really like the swimming pool all that much, but you loved the sea. You especially liked the gentle waves that made you bob up an down and they would make you laugh.

There were some German families there and they couldn't get their five and six year old children to go in the sea, without floods of tears. They kept pointing to you and telling their children , "Look at that little English baby, he has no fear"!

Paper © MM's designs; blue calligraphy pen from the Zig Memory System; other pens by Royal Sovereign

CHRISTOPHER AT THE SEASIDE

★ Simple layouts are often the best. We found the perfect background paper, so we decided to keep things simple. Two pictures were cropped for variety.

★ For fun we copied the following clip art onto cream paper: starfish (No. 59), shells (Nos. 60 and 61), seahorse (No. 62), bucket and spade (Nos. 63 and 64) and sandcastle (No. 65).

SWIMMING LESSONS

★ The right commercial paper can do much of the work for you. With this one we trimmed away the blank centre (around overlapping objects).

★ Photos were mounted on yellow paper then inserted into the opening. The journaling was also mounted on colourful matts.

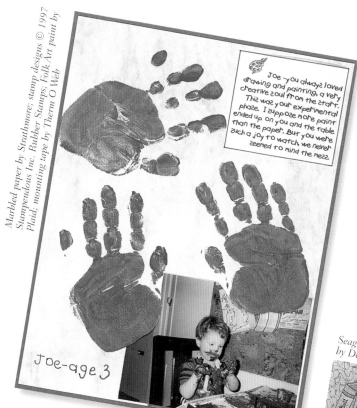

Marbled paper by Strathmore; stamp designs © 1997 Stampendous Inc. Rubber Stamps; Folk Art paint by Plaid; mounting tape by Therm O Web

Joe - you always loved drawing and painting, a very creative soul from the start. This was your experimental phase. I suppose more paint ended up on you and the table than the paper. But you were such a joy to watch we never seemed to mind the mess.

Joe-age 3

JOE PAINTING

★ How can you preserve your child's art or writing? Here's an idea. Help your child cover his or her hands in acrylic paint and then press them firmly on paper. Make lots of prints in different configurations so you have several to choose from.

★ A photo of the painting process creates a focus for the story. Here, parts of the prints have been cut away with a craft knife to slip the photo underneath.

★ For the final touch, get your child to write a few words or add your own words in his or her style.

Seagull, stamp scissors and heart punch by Fiskars; pencils by Derwent; Crafter's Pick Memory Mount Glue by api

STORYTIME

★ Aaron and Leanne loved listening to stories at the library, and we thought we'd make a feature of the time spent – and make a pun on 'storytime' – by creating this layout in the shape of a clock. We cropped the photos into circles using a circle cutter (see page 27) and then created the borders by mounting these on plain paper and trimming round them with decorative-edge scissors. We did the same for the centre of the clock.

★ The clock hands are strips of paper with small heart punches for the pointers.

★ The books (No. 32) and headphones (No. 35) are clip art. For a personalized touch, add the titles of your child's favourite story books to the spines of the copied books.

HOBBIES & LEISURE

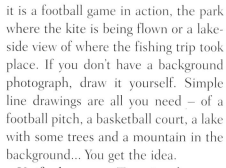

CHILDREN LIKE TO TRY OUT ALL SORTS OF DIFFERENT SPORTS AND ACTIVITIES. MANY ARE JUST A PASSING PHASE, OTHERS MAY BECOME A LIFE-LONG PASSION, BUT ALL ARE WORTH PRESERVING ON YOUR ALBUM PAGES.

Here are just a few suggestions for your leisure-activity pages.

* **Progress** Keep a record of your whole family's leisure-time activities. Follow the development of each hobby and include any new ones, however fleeting or unusual.

* **Background information** Include all relevant information on the hobby, sport or leisure activity featured on the page. Who, when, where, why and how did it start?

* **Set the scene** Include some of the surroundings to set the scene, whether it is a football game in action, the park where the kite is being flown or a lakeside view of where the fishing trip took place. If you don't have a background photograph, draw it yourself. Simple line drawings are all you need – of a football pitch, a basketball court, a lake with some trees and a mountain in the background... You get the idea.

* **Unify the pages** Try using the same border or page corners for all pages showing the development of a particular hobby. This will tie the pages together – and save time when planning new pages on the same theme.

* **Shapes, stamps and stickers** Use die-cut shapes, clip art, stamps and stickers to emphasize and enhance the theme. These are great for filling in blank spaces. You can also cut shapes from cards and stick them on or create little drawings or paintings yourself to embellish the page.

* **Certificates** Include awards, certificates and photos of any trophies where possible. You could even make a record of certificates and awards by colour photocopying them and reducing them in size. This makes them more manageable and leaves the originals free to be framed and hung on the wall.

GO-CARTING

★ *We loved making the background paper which set the scene on this page. We used a damp kitchen sponge to dab mud brown acrylic paint lightly over the paper at random. When this was dry we put a little paint on a paper plate and ran the front wheels of a toy truck through the paint and then over the paper – kids love to help with this one.*

Deborah, Gavin and
Graeme take a
turn at the wheel!

North Yorkshire - Christmas
1994

AARON FISHING

★ *This trip was a 'first' and featured a favourite hobby. We used a fairly simple blue background paper to suggest the blue of the sea – by choosing a simple design you can be sure that you can use it for any future layouts on the same theme without fear of it clashing with the pictures.*

★ *We kept the layout simple, using clip art to emphasize the theme – large fish (No. 53), small fish (No. 54), fishing rod (No. 55), splash (No. 56) and school of fish (No. 58).We photocopied these onto white and cream paper and lightly coloured in a few for variety.*

Paper by MPR Associates Inc.; Crafter's Pick Memory Mount Glue by api; pencils by Derwent

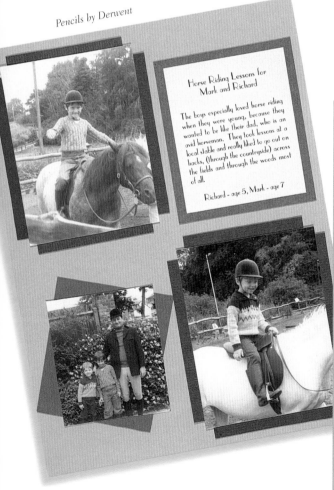

Pencils by Derwent

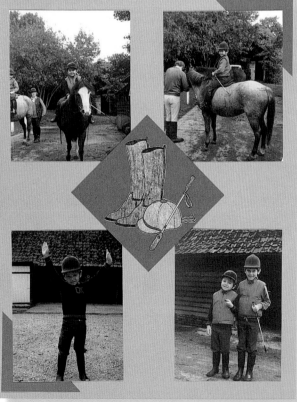

Paper from Hot Off the Press; stamps and ink © 1997 Stampendous Inc. Rubber Stamps

CAROUSEL

★ We wanted to capture all the fun of the fair in this layout, as well as the sparkle and night-time glitter of the occasion, so we used a vibrant background paper.

★ The decorative fairground horse is clip art No. 20 photocopied onto white paper and coloured in with markers. We also cut a bow from a second clip-art carousel horse to go at the top of the wording. The decorative corner pieces were cut from photographs of one of the ornate carousel benches.

Paper from MPR Associates Inc.; pencils by Derwent

LEANNE LEARNS NEEDLECRAFTS (right)

★ These photos were taken at different times and they were all different sizes so we made them more uniform by cropping them in the same shape.

★ Decorative paper and clip art fill the gaps. We copied the scissors (clip art No. 23), sewing basket (No. 24) and sewing machine (No. 25) onto white paper and coloured them in.

RIDING LESSONS (left)

★ A hobby which runs in the family is an ideal subject – in years to come, Mark and Richard will be delighted to see how they followed their father into the saddle.

★ Use up paper scraps for matts and page corners. The riding gear is coloured-in clip art No. 36.

Stamps and pigment ink © 1997 Stampendous Inc. Rubber Stamps

FEBRUARY 1991

THE COUSINS TOGETHER IN MESA, ARIZONA USA

MESA CITY PARK

SUPERSTITION SPRINGS MALL CHILDRENS PARK

LEANNE, CHRISTOPHER AND AARON AGES- 9, 4 AND 11

Pen by Royal Soverign; Crafter's Pick Memory Mount Glue by api

U 2 R Champs!

A Bit of Friendly BOXING! Mark and Richard February 1981

COUSINS IN ARIZONA

★ There were so many different things going on here and so many good photos to choose from that we let the pictures determine the design.

★ We included a fair bit of the background to set the scene, and because the pictures had so much going on, we kept the layout simple. We filled the blank areas with wording and stamping.

BOXING CHAMPS

★ This simple but eye-catching layout speaks for itself. We designed our own alphabet for the wording, photocopying the letters onto coloured paper, then cut them out and glued them on.

WINNERS' CUP

★ Record the day your child wins a competition with a layout like this. We cut round the picture of Joe holding the trophy to draw attention to him, then we filled in the gaps with clip art – No. 39 for the trophy, No. 40 for the football and No. 41 for the boots. (Even if you don't have a photo of the actual cup, you could still use the clip art to show who won the game).

★ Notice how the background helps to set the scene by echoing the design of the football strip.

Papers © the Paper Patch, pen by Royal Sovereign; pencils by Derwent

Paper by Hot Off the Press; pen by Royal Sovereign

KITE FLYING

★ Artworks – drawings, stickers or clip art – can set the scene or tell a story. We couldn't get a picture of Joe and the kite without moving very far away, so we added our own kite (clip art No. 17) to the close-up picture we had.

★ We drew a line to represent the string from the kite and cut it out with the kite, carefully positioning it so the string seems to come from Joe's hands without obscuring his face in any way.

★ We used a background paper which looked like a sky and copied the clouds, clip art Nos. 15 and 16, for the wording.

Paper by Hot Off the Press; pen from the Zig Memory System

SLAM DUNK

★ This layout shows that you can achieve a lot without necessarily spending hours over each page. The background paper shows what the story is about, and the title, written on a ball, slams it home.

★ Three of the pictures show Michael's skill with the ball and we couldn't resist the picture of him on a bike which shows his all-round sports ability.

FRIENDS

MANY OF LIFE'S EXPERIENCES — BOTH THE PEAKS AND THE TROUGHS — ARE SHARED WITH OUR FRIENDS. THEY ENJOY OUR HAPPINESS, CELEBRATE OUR SUCCESS, LISTEN TO OUR WOES AND SHARE OUR SORROW. IN YEARS TO COME YOU'LL WANT TO LOOK BACK AT HOW YOUR FRIENDSHIPS DEVELOPED OR REMEMBER FRIENDS YOU ONCE KNEW AND ALL THOSE EXPERIENCES YOU SHARED.

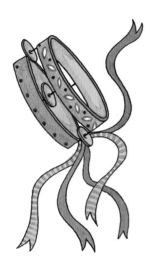

Each friend, whether fleeting or life-long, has played a part in what we are. Here are just a few ideas for how you can use a memory album to record and celebrate friendship.

• **Favourite things** Include your friend's favourite things on their page, such as foods, hobbies, sports or leisure activities.

• **How the friendship was formed** Tell the story of how you met and include experiences you've shared.

• **Make several pages** Create a collection of 'friendship' pages. Allocate a page or spread to each friend which includes photos and stories that capture his or her special qualities. By getting re-prints (or colour photocopies) you can make duplicates which you can give your friends to show them how much they mean to you.

• **Work together** Share the pleasure of creating a memory album with your friends. Work together on your individual albums. This is a great way to spend time together and be creative. You can share ideas as well as materials and tools. By making plans to work on your album with friends, you will be encouraged to make the time for this creative pastime, which can often be so easily postponed when day to day demands get in the way.

• **The gift of friendship** If a friend is moving away, make a friendship book as a going-away gift. Get other friends involved by letting them collect photographs from their own collections and create pages for the book. Again, reprints or colour photocopies are useful for making up duplicate pages as a memento for yourself.

CRAFT FRIENDS

★ *Sewing is the link – and bond – between the ladies on this page, so we created a layout that looks like a patchwork. We used fabric which a copy shop copied onto photo transfer paper for our background paper. (Usually photo transfer paper is used to copy pictures onto T-shirts etc.)*

★ *We printed the words from a computer, but all the other elements are clip art – the heart (basic shapes, page 110), wool, scissors, sewing basket, sewing machine, pins, thread, needles, tape measure, thimble and buttons (clip art Nos. 22-31).*

Watch Out! These Gals Are Crafty

There can be no happiness equal to the joy of finding a heart that understands.

THROUGH THE YEARS 1

★ *This spread (left and below) was designed to show the interaction between Debbie and Freida from their teen years through to marriages and families of their own. Although the background papers are different, they are designed to co-ordinate.*

★ *For the left-hand page we kept the pictures in basic rectangles but added a heart for the journaling for a change of pace.*

Paper © The Paper Patch; mini-scallop scissors by Fiskars; corner rounder by Marvy Uchida; stickers by Melissa Neufeld; pen by Royal Sovereign

THROUGH THE YEARS 2

★ To cover so many years of this friendship we wanted to use as many photographs as possible, so for the right-hand page we cropped some of the pictures quite small and cropped one in a circle for variety.

★ With so many photographs, each needed some explanation – use your own handwriting on a layout like this to show the message is from the heart.

Paper and scissors from Fiskars; pen from the Zig Memory System; Mono Adhesive by Tombow

FAMILY & FRIENDS

★ Using a selection of very similar papers for the background and matts creates quite a subtle yet decorative effect. We used three for this layout.

★ The circular photos were matted first with white paper which was cut with decorative-edge scissors then placed over the pin dot paper.

★ We glued down the photographs first followed by the lettering. Note down where the photographs were taken and who the people are.

SPECIAL FRIENDS

★ We used commercial and hand-made eraser stamps (see page 33) to decorate this page and to add the heading, name and date. The other wording is computer-generated.

★ The small triangles in each corner of the page were cut from coloured paper and glued on.

Stamp designs © 1997 Stampendous Inc. Rubber Stamps; marbled paper by Strathmore; Crafter's Pick Memory Mount Glue by api

ANIMAL FRIENDS

LIKE FRIENDS, ANIMALS PLAY AN IMPORTANT PART IN OUR LIVES. OUR PETS ARE PART OF OUR FAMILY AND THE LOVE AND COMPANIONSHIP SHARED BRING GREAT JOY. OTHER ANIMALS, LIKE THOSE WE SEE IN A ZOO, CAN BE FRIENDS FOR THE DAY OR 'ADOPTED' AS PART OF A LONGER ACQUAINTANCE.

If you like animals and have a pet or simply a favourite animal you'll want to include it in your album. You may also have made memorable visits to the zoo or a wildlife park or to a remote area where you have seen unusual animals or birds, like otters or puffins. Here are some suggestions to help you take suitable pictures for your album and some ideas for a few written details you may like to include.

• **Pedigree** If your pet has a pedigree or you know its history it's nice to record the details, such as the names of its parents, the date you got it, where you bought it, how old it was and how large and heavy.

• **Personality** Include your pet's likes, dislikes and favourites. What does he like to eat. Does she hate having a bath? What makes him excited? What makes her run away and hide? Try capturing these moments on film.

• **Tricks and habits** Be sure to photograph any special tricks or behaviour like a dog begging for a treat, a cat chasing its tail or an elephant cooling off by spraying water through its trunk.

• **Favourite places** Take photographs in different environments. Does your dog love to ride in the car with his head sticking out of the sunroof? Does your cat like to nap in a bed of ferns which catches the late morning sun? Does your bird like to hang upside down on its swing? Include any special personality traits as well as favourite haunts.

• **Family portraits** Be sure to include your pets in family photographs – after all, they are part of the family.

NOAH'S ARK

★ *This is a novel way of making a feature of a place visited. We used the complete photo and then cut just the group from another print of the picture to stick inside the fold-up clip art ark (No. 43).*

★ *For the fold-up ark we enlarged the clip art, then flipped it upside down and drew it again, this time adding the ramp. We cut out the shape of the joined ark and glued it on the page with the photo inside.*

★ *The cloud is drawn freehand, though you could use clip art No. 15. The animal decorations are stickers, placed in pairs, of course.*

A VISIT TO
NOAH'S ARK
SUMMER '84

BJ THE CAT

★ It's always nice to include details about your pet, like its date of birth, personality and habits, as in this layout, which concentrates on BJ as a kitten.

★ We emphasized the best picture by cutting it into an oval and mounting it on a rectangular matt. The scallops and border pattern are hand-drawn with coloured pens in terracotta and tan.

★ We cut the cat's name freehand from cream card because it was only two letters long, but you could use the letters from one of the alphabets on pages 122–123.

Pen from the Zig Memory System

MONKEY BUSINESS

★ We combined photographs from several visits to make this layout, so we felt they all needed captioning. To make the captions more interesting, we wrote on white paper rectangles, stuck them on yellow paper and then cut them out with decorative-edge scissors.

★ The monkeys, gorillas and bunch of bananas are all stickers.

Crafter's Pick Memory Mount Glue from api; stickers by Mrs. Grossman's ™ and Stickopotomus Inc. ™; yellow calligraphy pen from the Zig Memory System

JOE AND THE OWL

★ It's always fun to include mementos from a visit, particularly a really memorable one like this. We used some owl feathers, found on the ground when we met the owls of Whitbread Farm, Tunbridge, Kent, but you could use a pressed leaf from an autumn walk, a coin from a trip to a foreign country or even a ribbon from your daughter's hair.

★ Choose a few of your best photos for the page, and don't worry if some have unwanted backgrounds – just cut out the section you do want, like this fine owl.

OUR LITTLE FARMER

★ Most children love to visit animal parks where they can meet creatures close up. Because the pictures were good we framed them quite simply with plain brown matts and brightened up the page with clip art and stamped images.

★ The cow, sheep and chicken (clip art No. 45) were copied at 75% while the gate (No. 52) was reproduced full size. We cut the chicken away from the other animals to create a more natural group and to integrate the fence.

★ The sign for the animal park is tan paper appropriately cut to look like a piece of wood.

Paper by MPR Associates Inc.; brown calligraphy pen from the Zig Memory System; ink and stamp designs © 1997 Stampendous Inc. Rubber Stamps

Crafter's Pick Memory Mount Glue from api

Joe has always been fond of owls. Here at 3, he was so excited to show Grandad his new friend Barney. While visiting Whitbread Farm Tunbridge, Kent, his dream came true. Even though he was only 4, he was able to hold a real live owl. I'll never forget how proud he was.

Our Little Farmer

AZEVEDO FARMS

HOLIDAYS & VACATIONS

HOLIDAYS AND VACATIONS ARE GREAT TIMES TO GET LOTS OF TERRIFIC PHOTOGRAPHS OF FAMILY AND FRIENDS. WITH THE CHANGE IN OUR DAILY ROUTINE, AND HOPEFULLY WITHOUT OUR EVERYDAY STRESSES, WE ARE MORE RELAXED WHICH GENERALLY MAKES FOR MUCH BETTER PICTURES.

When holidays involve a trip from home you will want to capture memories of places visited and the unique experiences they created. And even if you stay close to home, you may well enjoy family fun which you want to remember. We have a few suggestions for how you can prepare for and capture the memories of any excursions, whether distant or not so far away.

• **Ever ready** Prepare ahead by having plenty of film and fresh batteries, and don't forget the camera.

• **More than you need** Take lots of photographs from many different angles and vary the distance from the subject. Remember, professional photographers take many photographs in order to get a few that they will use. Taking pictures from various different angles will provide more options for your page layouts.

• **Variety** Capture as much variety as possible. Include different forms of transport, the various areas and rooms of the hotel (outside the front door, swimming pool, dining room, lounge, reception, etc.), varying scenery, traffic in the streets (cars, buses, police cars and taxis), road signs, etc.

• **Spot the differences** When going abroad take photographs and jot down notes on those aspects of life which are interesting and different from your own lifestyle and environment such as different architecture, topography, flora and fauna, clothes styles, etc. These will help capture the essence of the places visited.

• **Collect memorabilia** Hold onto ticket stubs, travel brochures, maps, programmes, foreign money, etc. to use on your layouts. You can stick these on as in Joe and the Owl (page 69) or keep them in a pocket page or keeper envelope (see pages 36-39).

• **Keep notes** Jot down names and details at the end of each day. You'll be amazed at how quickly you can forget some of the important details you will want to include, such as place names or even good restaurants.

• **Double up** Where possible, it might be worth taking along two cameras. Cameras can break down – we have had more than our fair share – and it always seems to happen at the most important times.

TRAVEL JOURNAL

★ *This clipboard effect is a great way to use the maximum number of pictures from a trip and it enables you to include brief notes taken during the visit.*

★ *We arranged the pictures first to frame the page, then cut a rectangle from brown paper and rounded the corners for the clipboard backing. We rewrote the notes, using a different colour pen for each day, and then stapled them together. For the silver clip we cut out a piece of silver paper, punched out a hole and shaped the top with corner-edge scissors.*

KKID-TV

Jaffe's Travel Service
Our Travel Journal to:
The Pacific Northwest
11 & 14 July 1992

July 5 ~ Arrive in Seattle
attended Restaurant Food
Festival with Harold and Kim
July 6 ~ Tour and lunch at
the Space Needle. Took the
kids to the Science Museum
July 7 ~ Visit to Seattle Harbor
and Pikes Street Market
Dinner with the Jaffe's
July 8 ~ Train ride through
the mountains, drove up to

THE SNAPPER

AUTOGRAPHS

★ Create your own background paper using pens and markers, letting the style of the photos or layout dictate your design.
★ To make the autograph book, cut several pieces of paper in half. Stack them and fold in half then punch holes along the fold so you can insert the ribbon.

Scissors by Fiskars; pens from the Zig Memory System and Royal Sovereign

Paper by Hot Off the Press; stickers by Melissa Neufeld

AUGUST BY THE SEA

★ This mosaic background paper was quite busy, so we kept the layout simple, cropping the photos and shaping the edges with a rounded corner punch.
★ We added stickers for embellishment and added the words 'by the sea', cutting the letters from sandy areas of other photos using an alphabet we devised ourselves. We traced these backwards onto the back of the photos for a very clean cut.
★ The story was printed from a computer.

Summer 1986
This was Joe's first visit to the sea. We had a lovely family outing with Grandma Jo, Grandad, Graeme, and Stephen. It's hard to believe that just a year ago we were walking along this same beach and Joe was only a bump. My how our lives have changed.

Postcards ~ from the Edge

Marbled paper by Strathmore; stamp designs and inks © 1997 Stampendous Inc. Rubber
Stamps; ripple scissors by Fiskars; pen from the Zig Memory System

POSTCARDS FROM THE EDGE

★ *These simulated postcards make good mementoes. We cropped the photos and mounted them on white paper, trimmed with decorative-edge scissors.*

★ *We cut plain card in the same way with the space for the text in the message section and the location where the address goes.*

★ *We stamped on the postage stamp and the cancellation mark.*

SKIING IN ZERMATT

★ *Complement the bright colours of skiing gear with bright background colours, like the red and black used here. These colours also bring definition to the white snow background in the photographs.*

★ *We used a silver pen to write the text and echo the sparkle of the snow. The ski motifs are copies of clip art Nos. 67 and 68.*

EVERYDAY FUN

SOME OF OUR MOST PRECIOUS MEMORIES ARE OF EVERYDAY OCCURRENCES WHICH CAPTURE THE TRUE ESSENCE OF THOSE WE CARE ABOUT. AS OUR FAMILIES GROW OLDER, THEY DEVELOP AND CHANGE. HAVING A PHOTOGRAPHIC RECORD OF NORMAL DAILY ACTIVITIES WILL TAKE ON A SPECIAL MEANING IN YEARS TO COME.

Sometimes everyday events mean more than their face value. For example, a picture of your family playing Monopoly might remind you of the wheeler-dealer instinct of a son who grew up to be an estate agent. Having trouble with a teenager who is always on the phone? Perhaps all those photos of her on the phone as a child should have given you a clue.

Here are a few suggestions to help you balance the memories in your album with layouts of the day to day happenings in your family.

• **Traditions** Take photographs of everyday family traditions – fish and chips on Friday nights, playing board games on Saturday evenings or country rambles after large Sunday lunches.

• **Routines** Include photographs of normal family routines. Mealtimes can be fun, particularly if the whole family is together. Record the likes and dislikes of varying family members, like your son eating his favourite snacks. Playing in the park is a favourite for most families, and even visits to the library become special if your child has a passion for books.

• **Loaded** Keep your camera loaded with film (and extra rolls handy) and in a place where you can easily put your hands on it. What about keeping a disposable camera in the glove compartment of the car or a pocket of your coat? There are so many candid opportunities that are lost because we don't have a camera at the right moment.

• **Taken unawares** Candid shots are the most fun, especially when they portray the unique personality of the subject. A child's unique sleeping position or an adult's facial features when concentrating are examples of everyday things which will be treasured in years to come.

CHRISTOPHER EATING GRAPES

★ *Christopher has always loved grapes, and after this humorous event in his childhood when he offered up some half-eaten grapes to a guest, we wanted to record it.*

★ *We made the grapes by cutting ovals from light-green paper and lightly coloured them with a beige pen. We grouped them to make the bunch, raising some by adding small squares of foam tape to the back to create a three-dimensional effect. For fun we stamped a face on a few grapes.*

★ *The ivy, clip art No. 51, was copied onto tan paper, and coloured brown, then cut out and glued on.*

Grapes Anyone?

Christopher -
you were two years
old in these photos.

You always loved grapes and still do. I'll never forget the time Tony Cooper was over for tea. He saw how much you liked grapes and he told you he wished he had some too. You walked over to him very seriously, spit out the grapes you had in your mouth, and handed them to him. Mummy and Daddy were so embarassed, but Tony, Aunty Ivana, Mark and Richard collapsed in laughter.

JOE LOVES CONTAINERS

★ Joe loved bathing, and would willingly hop into even the smallest container of water, so we collected several pictures of him in his makeshift baths to make this layout.

★ We used several layers of co-ordinating papers for the matts, trimming the corners of some with corner edgers. We also used a mini heart punch to create more interest at the corners, and added further decoration with stickers.

Blue striped paper from Creative Papers by C.R. Gibson; Bryce and Madeline stickers from Melissa Neufeld Inc. © Jone Hallmark, available from First Class Stamps Ltd; cloud scissors and nostalgia corner edger from Fiskars; mini heart punch by McGill

WINTER FUN

★ Take advantage of background details like the houses in these photos by cutting around the top edges, silhouette-style. We attached our pictures to handmade background paper (see pages 24-25) and wrote the text in a circle for variety.

★ The snowflakes are clip art No. 66 photocopied and coloured in with metallic silver pen, then cut out with different decorative-edge scissors and glued on.

Scallop, cloud, volcano and peaks scissors from Fiskars; pens from the Zig Memory System and Royal Sovereign

Marbled paper by Strathmore; pens from the Zig Memory System

LOVE ON THE ROCKS

★ *We positioned the photos on the first page in each corner, trimming them to leave an empty oval. We filled the oval with a special picture – the figure is recognisable by the family.*

★ *We continued the same look on the second page but this time kept all the pictures rectangular.*

JAM SESSION

★ *Here we drew along the decorative edge of each ruler, indenting slightly into the edge of the paper. We used a rubber stamp embossing pen and gold embossing powder to create a raised effect, and then trimmed away the plain edge.*

★ *When attaching the decorative papers we didn't glue them along the left margin so mementoes could be inserted.*

★ *The musical notes (No. 75) and treble clef (No. 76) from the clip art were also embossed, as was the title.*

Embossing pen by Tsukineko; gold embossing powder © 1997 Stampendous Inc.; Rubber Stamps; gold photo corners by Canson; green pen from the Zig Memory System

DENNIS THE MENACE PARK

★ This colourful background paper is handmade – we stamped on plain paper with pencil erasers using bold pigment inks. If you wish, you can carve the erasers into different shapes (see page 33).

★ The pictures were cropped and then trimmed with a rounded corner edger; for the circular picture and matts we used a circle cutter, and for the heart-shaped photo and matts we used a template (page 110). We trimmed the middle matts of the two centre photos with decorative-edge scissors. The colourful layers under the remaining photos are just triangles shaped with a corner rounder.

Pens from the Zig Memory System; volcano and mini-pinking scissors from Fiskars; ink from Stampendous Inc.

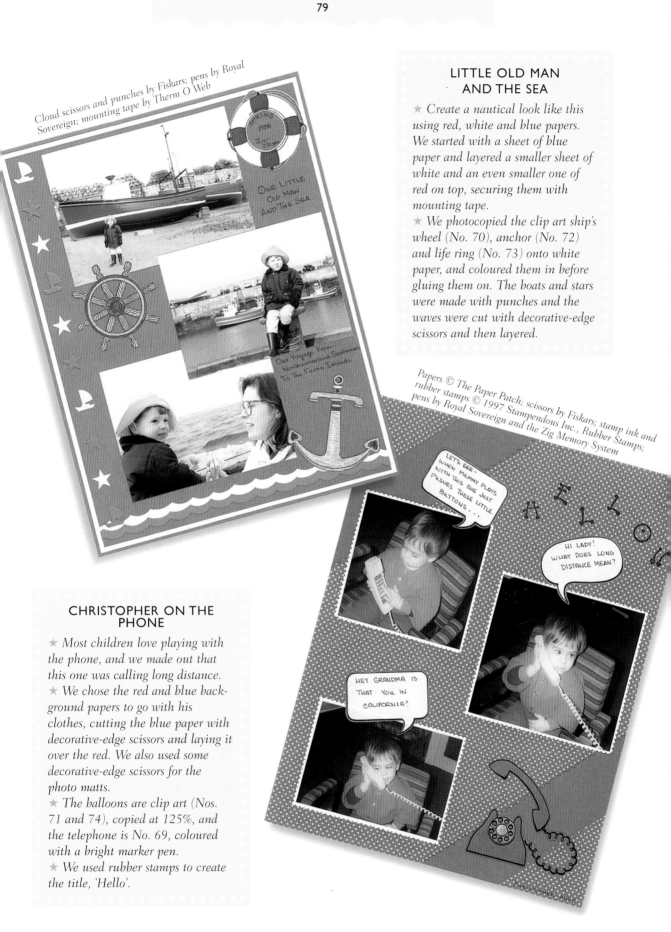

Cloud scissors and punches by Fiskars; pens by Royal Sovereign; mounting tape by Therm O Web

LITTLE OLD MAN AND THE SEA

★ Create a nautical look like this using red, white and blue papers. We started with a sheet of blue paper and layered a smaller sheet of white and an even smaller one of red on top, securing them with mounting tape.

★ We photocopied the clip art ship's wheel (No. 70), anchor (No. 72) and life ring (No. 73) onto white paper, and coloured them in before gluing them on. The boats and stars were made with punches and the waves were cut with decorative-edge scissors and then layered.

Papers © The Paper Patch; scissors by Fiskars; stamp ink and rubber stamps © 1997 Stampendous Inc., Rubber Stamps; pens by Royal Sovereign and the Zig Memory System

CHRISTOPHER ON THE PHONE

★ Most children love playing with the phone, and we made out that this one was calling long distance.

★ We chose the red and blue background papers to go with his clothes, cutting the blue paper with decorative-edge scissors and laying it over the red. We also used some decorative-edge scissors for the photo matts.

★ The balloons are clip art (Nos. 71 and 74), copied at 125%, and the telephone is No. 69, coloured with a bright marker pen.

★ We used rubber stamps to create the title, 'Hello'.

SPECIAL DAYS

THERE ARE ALL SORTS OF SPECIAL DAYS YOU WILL WANT TO RECORD IN YOUR ALBUM, SUCH AS A FRIEND'S WEDDING, A CHRISTENING OR OTHER RELIGIOUS CELEBRATION, A GRADUATION OR COMING-OF-AGE CELEBRATION, OR EVEN JUST A BIRTHDAY OR ANNIVERSARY OF SOME KIND.

Here are a few pointers to help you make plans for the next special day.

• **Share photos** At family occasions where several people are taking pictures, why not arrange to share with each other? That way you will have lots more photographs to choose from – and so will your friends if they also enjoy making photo albums.

• **Several cameras** At large, important events where there are lots of people, like a relative's wedding, why not pass round several disposable cameras to people who haven't brought one with them so that every aspect of the occasion will be covered. Remember, at crowded events you may not always be able to get a good view – but perhaps a friend can.

• **Presents** Where there is gift giving, take photographs of the presents as they are unwrapped. Jot down who gave what for more detailed journaling. Both the gift-giver and the recipient will be glad of a photographic record.

• **Cards and flowers** Include memorabilia to help focus on the occasion. A few pressed flowers from the bridal bouquet, for example, the invitation for a birthday party or a piece of lace from the christening gown could be included on page layouts for special days. Pocket pages and keeper envelopes are safe ways of preserving such memorabilia.

• **Record people's thoughts** For the journaling for an occasion like a wedding or christening, include a few words about the event or the subject from each family member. If you are feeling ambitious, add a sentence from each important guest.

LISA'S WEDDING

★ *To create this stylish layout, first photocopy your cutwork design – we used the ribbon (No. 89) from the clip art section, photocopying it at 125%. Tape it in position over the top paper – ours was off-white – and cut through the copy and paper with a sharp craft knife very carefully. (You can trim rough edges afterwards with scissors.) Use a cutting mat to protect your work surface.*

★ *Now centre the photo on the paper and mark a border 1cm (½in) larger all round; cut it out. Finally trim the edges of the paper and lay it on a sheet of contrasting paper, sticking the picture in the middle.*

CHRISTOPHER'S FIRST CAR

★ *A layout like this would make a wonderful thank-you present for the giver.*

★ *We used quite a bit of clip art for this layout. The garland (No. 77), wreath (No. 79), holly (No. 80) and gift (No. 84) were all copied onto white paper and coloured in. The stocking (No. 78) was reduced in size so it would fit the layout by photocopying it at 75%.*

★ *Notice that we stuck the gift on a double oval matt, and trimmed the outer one with decorative-edge scissors to add to the festive feel.*

Paper © The Paper Patch; pen from the Zig Memory System

Mini-scallop and colonial scissors by Fiskars; pens from the Zig Memory System and from Royal Sovereign

THE GREATEST GIFT *(left)*

★ *This simple but effective layout takes its colour from the smashing Santa outfit the baby is wearing. The plain red matts define the pictures and emphasize the colour.*

★ *We used the holly (No. 80) and gift (No. 84) from the clip art section, photocopying them onto white paper so we could colour them in before we stuck them in place on the page.*

HALLOWEEN

★ The story was the feature of this occasion, so we printed ours on cream paper to ensure it was neat and easy to read. Then we mounted it on a single matt to give it more weight.

★ We cut out the pumpkins and wooden crates from the photos for variety and to remove unwanted detail from the photographs.

Paper from Hot Off the Press; Bryce and Madeline stickers from Melissa Neufeld Inc. © Jone Hallmark, available from First Class Stamps Ltd

Papers and pens from the Zig Memory System and Royal Sovereign; corner punch by Family Treasures

GRADUATION

★ Using multiple matts helps to give an important picture like this more weight. The inner cream matt is 3mm (⅛in) larger than the photo, the first black matt is 6mm (¼in) larger than that, and the big cream matt is 6mm (¼in) larger still. Finally the large black matt is 8mm (⅜in) larger and has been trimmed with a decorative corner edger.

Leather-look paper from Hot Off the Press; bandanna paper by Frances Meyer Inc. ™; volcano scissors by Fiskars

Christopher's 6th Birthday

He chose a western theme for his party because he was so proud of being half American and to him American meant, cowboys and indians. Christopher also liked the restaurant and wanted a party where he could invite lots of friends. There were 19 children in all and 6 adults! We all had a lot of fun, especially Uncle Brian and Daddy. It looks like they've had a little too much root beer.

Paper and deckle scissors by Fiskars; floral stickers by Mrs. Grossman's ™; Uni-ball pen by Royal Sovereign

Grandma's 80th Birthday

SURPRISE !!

Grandma's Girls

October 3, 1990

WILD-WEST BIRTHDAY PARTY

★ We found the ideal background paper for this wild-west party but decided to jazz it up further by using the outer edge of another paper as a frame.

★ We cut the circular picture with a circle cutter (see page 27) and placed it on a marshal's badge (clip art No. 34 traced onto silver paper) over a circular red matt trimmed with decorative-edge scissors.

★ The boots (No. 37) and hat (No. 38) are clip art too.

ROLLER COASTER (right)

★ Cut-outs of pictures always add life and dynamism to a page. By cutting two of the pictures in silhouette and laying them on a rolling track (drawn by hand) we were able to capture the excitement of the ride.

★ We decorated the second page by layering pink paper over blue and adding hearts made with a punch. The large hearts were cut using a template (see page 110) and then trimmed with decorative-edge scissors (see page 26).

★ The cloud is clip art No. 16 and the banner is No. 88.

GRANDMA'S 80TH BIRTHDAY

★ We trimmed the edge of this background paper with decorative-edge scissors for variety and used a rounded corner edger to neaten the rectangular pictures. To give the oval pictures a framed look we cut two simple rectangular matts to go underneath each one.

★ Stickers add the final touch.

Scissors and punch by Fiskars

It's a good thing Joe finished that ice cream cone before we rode on this ride!

Chessington Land of Adventures 1988

Mummy and Joe ~ 3 yr.

CHRISTMAS FIREPLACE

★ We created the brick pattern on this page by cutting narrow strips of dark red paper with a trimmer and gluing them on in a staggered brick pattern. We glued the sides and bottom to a sheet of paper so we could slip mementoes inside.

★ The garland (no. 77), stocking (No. 78) and wreath (No. 79) are clip art. We copied the wreath and garland at 110% and the stocking at about 50% to fit our layout, colouring them in with markers before gluing them in place. Notice that we cut away the toys from the stocking copies.

Paper trimmer by Fiskars; marbled paper by Strathmore Inc.; pens by Royal Sovereign and the Zig Memory System

Papers © The Paper Patch; corner rounder by Royal Sovereign; silver pen by Marvy Uchida; mounting tape by Therm O Web

HEIDI'S CHRISTENING

★ We used a large square acid-free paper doily to decorate this page, turning it on the diagonal to create a diamond shape.

★ The cross is clip art No. 85 photocopied onto white paper, coloured in with a silver pen and then mounted on a small matt in co-ordinating paper.

CHRISTOPHER'S CHRISTENING

★ For this layout we photocopied the lace frame on page 100 onto white paper, then cut out the photocopied frame about 6mm (¼in) from the edge. We glued this towards the top of another sheet of white paper, then photocopied it onto cream paper and coloured the aperture edge with felt tips.

★ We hand wrote the details at the bottom in black pen, decorating it with flowers, leaves and tendrils. Then we mounted the page onto large sheets of coloured paper.

Le Plume pigmented markers by Marvy Uchida; Mono Adhesive by Tombow

Papers by HyGloss; gold pen by Royal Sovereign; Class A Peels ™ sticker accents by Mark Enterprises; deckle scissors by Fiskars

50TH WEDDING ANNIVERSARY

★ The obvious colour for the backing paper for a golden wedding anniversary is gold, so that's what we chose here. We trimmed the edge of another paper with decorative-edge scissors to go on top as a base for the pictures.

★ The small keeper envelope houses confetti from the reception tables (see page 37 for further details).

Paper by Geopaper; mini-scallop scissors by Fiskars; gold pen by Royal Sovereign

ENGAGEMENT TO WEDDING

★ This spread tells the story of a couple from engagement through to wedding.

★ Because the chemicals from newspaper print can damage photos, we used buffer matts to protect the photo from the clipping. Each page will be kept in a page protector, isolating the newsprint from other photos in the album.

CHRISTOPHER'S GODPARENTS

★ This layout uses the heart template from page 106. We photocopied it onto coloured paper and coloured in the small hearts with felt-tip pens.

★ We cut our photographs to fit into the heart shapes and glued them on, then traced around the photos with black marker pen for definition. We cut smaller hearts from black paper for our journaling.

Pens from the Zig Memory System and by Royal Sovereign; Mono Adhesive by Tombow

FAMILIES

MANY OF THE PAGES WE HAVE BEEN TALKING ABOUT ARE MADE UP OF FAMILY PHOTOGRAPHS, OFTEN FOCUSING ON A SPECIAL OCCASION. BUT THERE MAY BE TIMES WHEN YOU WANT TO CREATE A PAGE WHICH ISN'T FOCUSED ON ANY SPECIFIC EVENT. PERHAPS YOU SIMPLY WANT TO RECOGNISE THE LIFE OR A TIME IN THE LIFE OF A PARTICULAR FAMILY MEMBER, A COUPLE OR BROTHERS AND SISTERS.

It's fun to create pages which focus on an individual or which compare different family members as we did in the page layouts below. How many times have you heard someone say your toddler looks just like his dad or grandfather at a similar age? Think how special it would be to have a page showing this. Another form of comparison which can be very effective on a spread is a child's development through to adulthood.

Families are what the best memories are all about, so preserve those precious moments with photographs and page layouts, lovingly planned and created by someone who cares.

COUSINS

★ *Two sets of photos showing cousins on both sides of the family made this spread possible.*
★ *Just simple matting using two printed papers proved quite effective.*

NAVY DAYS

★ To jazz up these black-and-white photos of Grandpa in the Navy, we mounted a striped paper over a plain paper.

★ We used colour photocopies so we could retain the sepia tone in these photos from the 1950s. Under the silhouette there is a triple matt of light grey, charcoal grey and black. The oval-shaped photos have single matts, while the square and partially silhouetted flag and movie screen have double matts (see page 19).

Pens from the Zig Memory System

Lifeboat · USS Onslow · 1951

Navy buddies · Alabama · Schrader · and others · Japan · 1952

Movie Screen · USS Onslow

San Diego California

Bernie Vertrees 1950

Papers by Hot Off the Press

THE VERTREES FAMILY

★ This is a great way to use proofs from a photo sitting.

★ Trim the edges of a piece of patterned paper and glue it onto plain paper – here the paper matches the background in the photos. By cutting out the desired shape from the printed paper, photos mounted behind can remain intact.

1913

This is the wedding photo of my grandparents, Earl Smith and Maude DeGraw who were married on Christmas Eve. This also happened to be my grandfathers birthday. One of his favorite meals was oyster stew and Granny would make it for him every year on his birthday. It became an annual tradition and even though Grandpa Earl is no longer with us, the tradition continues with the family to this day.

MY GRANDPARENTS

★ Don't forget some of those great old black-and-white photos, but don't use the original in your albums – have colour photocopies made which are almost as good.

★ We found wonderful papers for this layout, so all we had to do was add the text, which was computer-generated. We shaped the matts with corner edgers.

Background paper from Hot Off the Press; marbled paper by Strathmore

ODD PHOTOGRAPHS

THERE MAY BE TIMES WHEN YOU DON'T HAVE ENOUGH PHOTOS OF ONE OCCASION TO MAKE UP A STORY OR PAGE LAYOUT. AT OTHER TIMES YOU MAY FIND YOU HAVE ODD PHOTOS WHICH ARE TOO PRECIOUS TO THROW OUT, BUT DON'T REALLY SEEM TO HANG TOGETHER WITH ANY OTHER PICTURES. HERE'S HOW TO USE THEM.

The best way to show how you can use odd photos is by example. On Busy Boy (below) you can see how pictures can show a developing personality.

BUSY BOY

★ By using two co-ordinating prints you can vary the background design yet still create a pleasing look on a spread.
★ We cropped these pictures in circles using a circle cutter (see page 27), although you could choose any shape, even simple squares. We had a few pictures that didn't fit in a circle, so we put the flat edge against the edge of the paper as if they were meant to be that way. This works very well.
★ The matts are trimmed with decorative-edge scissors and the little shapes are punches.

Leanne was fascinated by the telephone since she was very little. Now she is in her teens, she spends every possible moment on the telephone so we chose some of the best pictures to create our layout (right).

Aaron is known for his passion for cars. So it was no surprise when we found a collection of photographs of Aaron at different ages, all with wheels. They combine to make a light-hearted spread (far right). You could create a similar look choosing any pictures with a common thread – a child eating a favourite food, reading or whatever is appropriate.

Scissors and punches by Fiskars; pen from the Zig Memory System

WHEELS *(right)*

★ Since we entitled this layout 'Wheels', we cropped most of the photos in circles of different sizes and followed the shape with the captions. We added stickers and a punched bicycle shape for embellishment. The title is stamped on.

Stamp designs and inks © 1997 Stampendous Inc.;
Rubber Stamps; stickers by Mrs. Grossman's ™

Paper, scissors and corner edger by Fiskars; stickers by Mrs.
Grossman's ™; computer font is Fontastic by DJ Inkers

I'LL GET IT! *(left)*

★ When we ran across the little photo of Leanne as a toddler on the phone we knew we had to make a page of it. Even though the quality is poor, the action is still apparent and adds so much to the page. We emphasized this picture by giving it a double matt, cropping the matts with corner edgers for decoration.

★ We copied the clip-art telephone (No. 69) at 125% onto white paper and then coloured it in with pencils. We used stamps for the lettering and punched hearts and stickers of phones to complete the page.

Papers © The Paper Patch; stamp designs and ink © 1997 Stampendous
Inc.; stickers by Mrs. Grossman's ™; scissors and punch by Fiskars

GREAT GRANDMA ALVES

★ We let the memorial window dictate what colours to use on this page. We created the double and triple matts by cutting coloured paper slightly larger than the photo or text and trimming some with decorative-edge scissors. Even the text picks up on the colours of the window.

★ We created the corner pieces by cutting them with a corner edger. The flowers are all stickers.

CREATIVE ALBUM COVERS

HAVING SPENT A LOT OF TIME CREATING ATTRACTIVE ALBUM PAGES, YOU'LL WANT SOMEWHERE NICE TO DISPLAY THEM. A PLAIN PHOTO ALBUM JUST DOESN'T SEEM SPECIAL ENOUGH. HERE ARE SOME IDEAS FOR MAKING AND DECORATING YOUR OWN ALBUMS.

DECORATIVE ALBUMS

To decorate a plain binder, cover it in fabric (see opposite), découpage it or stencil it. To make your own hand-made album like the little punch-bound album below turn to page 94.

The easiest way to create an attractive album is to buy a plain one and decorate it. If you are going to cover it completely with paper, fabric or other items you can save money by buying a plain, inexpensive album. However, if you happen to find an album you like the look of, you can keep your decorations to a minimum, just adding a few touches to personalize it.

• **Fabric-covered album** This is one of the nicest and simplest ways to decorate an album and it means you can choose a fabric to suit the themes of your album pages. For example, if it's going to feature your children you could choose a bold children's print fabric, while if it is a wedding and anniversary album you could cover it in raw silk or even with a remnant of your wedding-dress fabric. For a special touch, embroider the fabric first. For a luxurious look, glue wadding to the album before attaching the fabric. Full instructions for covering a photo album in fabric are given opposite.

• **Découpage** Another simple idea is to cover the album with shapes cut from photos, colour photocopies, wrapping paper and cards – anything associated with the pages in the album. You can even add some journaling, printed from a computer or hand written. Simply arrange all the pieces on your album and glue them in place with strong glue. To protect the paper shapes and to prevent them rubbing off, apply a few coats of varnish. Alternatively, use a crackle-glaze kit, available from art shops, to give it an aged look.

• **Stencilling** This is best done on a card album as the paint may not adhere to a plastic cover. Paint the whole cover first to provide a base, if you wish, then stencil your design on top, using a stencilling brush for a soft effect or a sponge for a romantic, cloudy look. If you prefer, you can stencil onto paper or thin card, cut it to fit your album and then glue it in place.

Making a Fabric-covered Binder

1 If using wadding cut it to fit the album and glue it on. Now cut a fabric rectangle 5cm (2in) larger all round than the album. Cut two pieces of card 6mm (¼in) shorter and narrower than the inside front cover of the album. Then cut two fabric pieces 2.5cm (1in) larger all round than each card piece which you will use later to cover them.

2 Lay the album centrally over the wrong side of the fabric rectangle. Mark each edge of the spine on the fabric then mark 1cm (½in) away from the first marks. Clip the fabric allowance at the second set of marks. Fold over the fabric between the clips and glue down, fabric to fabric. Repeat to glue down the flap at the opposite end of the spine.

3 Glue the fabric to the album, starting at the corners, as shown. Glue cord, lace, braid or any other trim around the outside edge of the album. Finally, cover and glue the card inside the album to cover the fabric edges. Insert a tassel or ribbon loop as a handle, if desired.

MAKING YOUR OWN ALBUM

ALTHOUGH THERE ARE ALL SORTS OF ALBUMS AVAILABLE READY-MADE, THERE MAY COME A TIME WHEN YOU CAN'T FIND QUITE WHAT YOU ARE LOOKING FOR. YOU MIGHT WANT A PARTICULARLY SMALL ALBUM TO HOUSE A SET OF PICTURES, FOR EXAMPLE, OR YOU COULD NEED A REALLY LARGE ONE. HERE'S WHAT YOU CAN DO.

MOSAIC ALBUM
Whether the album you choose is ready-made or handmade, you can have fun decorating it. Glue a feature photograph to the centre of the cover, and attach decorative sticky-backed jewel shapes all around it to create a mosaic pattern.

Making your own album is not as difficult as it sounds. With some stiff card and paper you can make a stunning pocket-sized album like the one shown opposite. Or if you wish to work on a larger scale you can make a pretty punch-bound album from board and decorate it however you please.

Making your own album means you can decide on your own format – large square pages, for example, or short, wide ones to accommodate panoramic pictures. You are only limited by the size of your materials.

• **Concertina album** By folding a sheet of paper concertina style and gluing your pictures inside you can create a quick pocket-sized album (see opposite). We used black paper as the base for ours because it's a traditional colour for album pages and it goes with most pictures. For added decoration, cut picture mounts from coloured paper in simple or crazy shapes and glue your pictures behind them before attaching them to the album. Then add a few embellishments to the front.

• **Punch-bound album** If you'd like a more substantial album you can make one by folding board into the shape you require for the cover, remembering to include a spine down the middle. You'll get neater results if you score your fold lines lightly with a craft knife before you bend the board. Cover the album with fabric, découpage or paper before adding the album pages. Cut your pages slightly smaller than the album so they will be protected and punch holes in one edge.

Thread jute string or ribbon through the holes of the album and the pages so you can tie the ends together on the front in a neat bow or knot. For strength, thread the string through each hole twice before securing it.

Making a Concertina Album

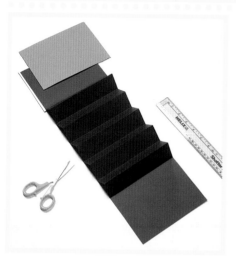

To decorate the front cover and inside covers, cut a star shape from decorative paper. Crop the photographs into small circles and mount in the centre of the stars. Glue in position, then add your text and embellish with stickers.

1   Cut two 13 x 18cm (5 x 7in) pieces of board. Cut one 64 x 16.5cm (25 x 6½in) piece of stiff black acid-free paper. Fold the paper in a concertina as follows. Measure 12cm (4¾in) and fold; measure 4cm (1½in) and fold back; measure 4cm (1½in) and fold up. Continue folding every 4cm (1½in) until you have 10 folds, then measure 12cm (4¾in) and trim away any excess, if necessary.

2   Glue two 25cm (10in) pieces of ribbon halfway down the long inside edges of both matt board pieces. Glue each of the 12cm (4¾in) portions of the black paper to the insides of the matt board pieces (over the ribbon).

3   Cut pairs of hearts, ovals, rectangles with oval apertures, rectangles with rectangular apertures and cameras from coloured paper. Glue your photographs behind them. Finally, glue the photos back to back into the concertina album.

OTHER OPTIONS

BY NOW YOU'LL HAVE A PRETTY GOOD IDEA HOW TO CREATE EYE-CATCHING PAGES IN YOUR ALBUMS AND MAY WELL BE STARTING TO THINK ABOUT OTHER WAYS OF PUTTING YOUR DESIGN IDEAS TO GOOD USE. THIS CHAPTER GIVES SOME PRACTICAL SUGGESTIONS FOR HOW YOU CAN USE THE IDEAS IN THIS BOOK IN OTHER WAYS.

Use these suggestions to spark off your imagination and own ideas.

• **Recipe book** Most families have favourite recipes that become tradition from year to year – a special soup on Christmas day, a favourite birthday cake or a particular wedding dish, for example. You can make these recipes even more special by mounting them in an album, adding photographs and perhaps telling the story of where the recipe first came from or describing an association it has. Why not make copies for all the cooks in the family or create an album of recipes for a bride just starting out?

• **Calendar** A calendar is much nicer if it's personal, so it's an appealing idea to make your own using your favourite photographs. Either create one page and attach your yearly calendar to the bottom – a ready-made one or one you've drawn up yourself – or create one page for every month of the year. You could feature a member of the family on each page or use photos of places where you've had good holidays at that time of year.

• **Alphabet book** Young children love to recognize familiar images in pictures, so think how exciting they would find a book showing all their favourite things. They will learn their letters in no time if you create a book of the alphabet which includes them and their best-loved things.

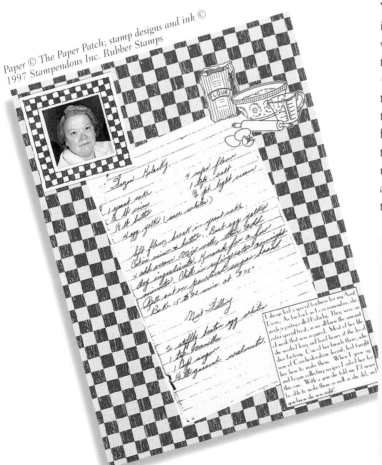

Paper © The Paper Patch; stamp designs and ink © 1997 Stampendous Inc. Rubber Stamps

FAVOURITE RECIPE

★ *My aunt who inspired this page always wrote on small notebooks. She had beautiful handwriting, so we photocopied a page from her cookbook onto tan paper along with the clip art (No. 33) and printed the text on the same paper.*

★ *The simple chequered background paper seemed to go with the picture and adds the traditional look we wanted.*

A IS FOR ALY

★ This shows how you can decorate a page in an alphabet book. All the letters and the borders are stencilled on, the anchor is a die-cut shape and the arrow is a strip of paper with a punched heart for a pointer. All the other decorations are stickers, except for the ants which we drew ourselves.

Stencils and paints by American Traditional Stencils and C-Thru Ruler Company; die cut by Creative Memories; heart punch by Fiskars; stickers by Frances Meyer Inc. ™ and Stickopotomus Inc. ™; pen from the Zig Memory System

B IS FOR BEN

★ There's plenty going on here to draw the eye, and each item is labelled, so as children get older they will be able to read the words.
★ We cropped and attached the pictures first, leaving space for the initial letter at the top.
★ We stamped the chequerboard frame in the top corner and used stamps for the letters too.
★ Small rubber stamps and stickers fill in the gaps.

Patterns and...

A face without
freckles, is like
a sky without
stars!

Leanne
age 4

Heart
To Heart
Chat

Leanne

Dave

CONTENTS

...templates...

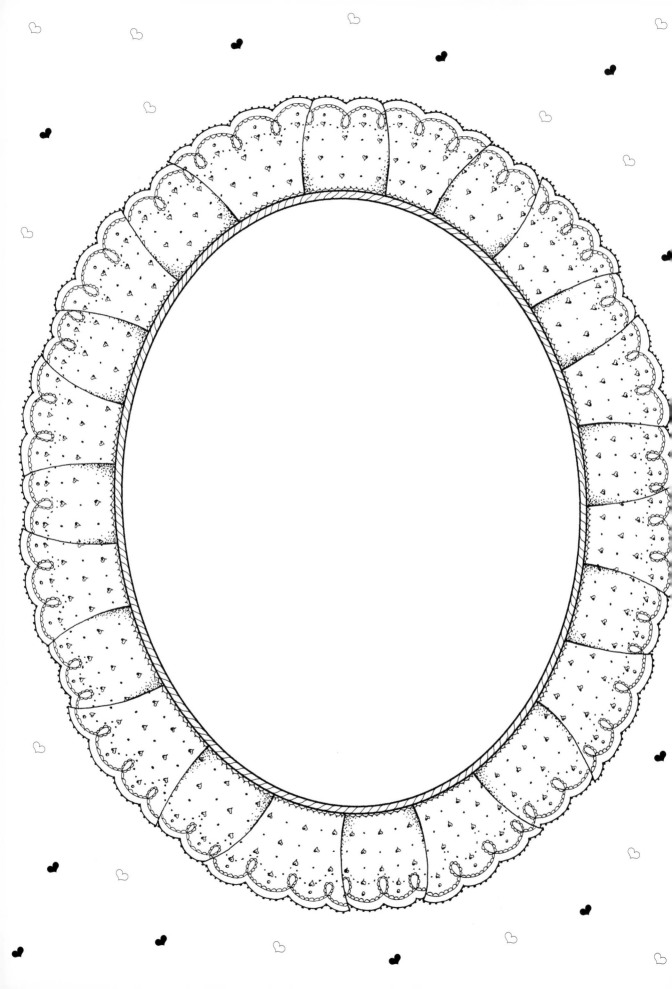

LACE FRAME ..... A FRAME FOR A SPECIAL PORTRAIT.

HANNAH

★ Photocopy the template opposite onto white paper at 95%.

★ Photocopy the bow, clip art No. 6 onto pink paper.

★ Colour the braid around the oval aperture in pink, then carefully cut out the frame and stick it onto blue paper.

★ Crop the photograph to fit over the aperture.

★ Punch hearts from pink paper and glue them randomly around the oval. Glue the bow in place.

BRIDE

★ Photocopy the template opposite onto pale pink paper. Cut a strip from each side and layer over moss-green paper.

★ Colour the braid on the oval with a green felt pen.

★ Crop the picture to fit over the central aperture and glue it in place or cut out the centre of the oval and put your picture behind it so your picture stays intact.

★ Glue a bow to the bottom.

STARS ....

USE THIS TEMPLATE TO SHOW WHAT A STAR YOUR CHILD IS.

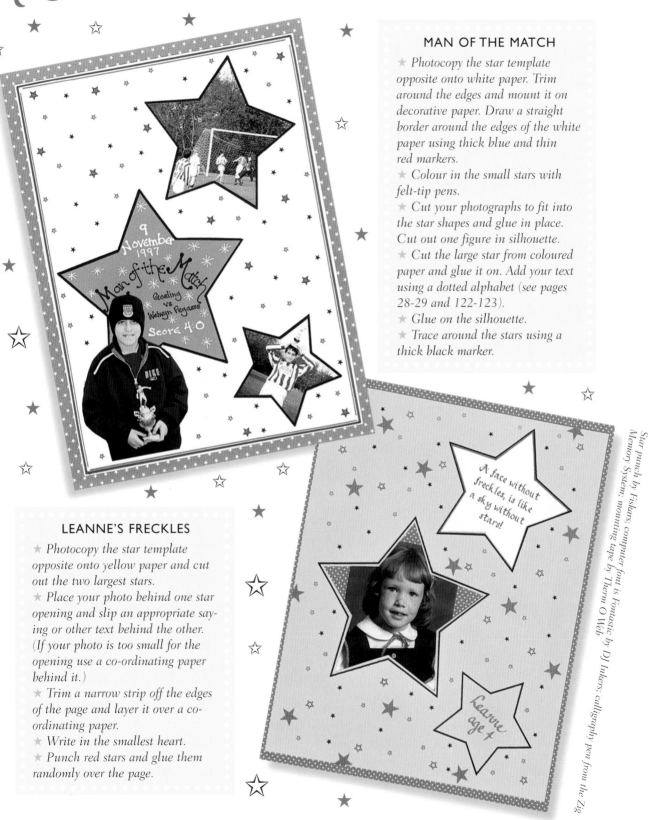

MAN OF THE MATCH

★ Photocopy the star template opposite onto white paper. Trim around the edges and mount it on decorative paper. Draw a straight border around the edges of the white paper using thick blue and thin red markers.

★ Colour in the small stars with felt-tip pens.

★ Cut your photographs to fit into the star shapes and glue in place. Cut out one figure in silhouette.

★ Cut the large star from coloured paper and glue it on. Add your text using a dotted alphabet (see pages 28-29 and 122-123).

★ Glue on the silhouette.

★ Trace around the stars using a thick black marker.

LEANNE'S FRECKLES

★ Photocopy the star template opposite onto yellow paper and cut out the two largest stars.

★ Place your photo behind one star opening and slip an appropriate saying or other text behind the other. (If your photo is too small for the opening use a co-ordinating paper behind it.)

★ Trim a narrow strip off the edges of the page and layer it over a co-ordinating paper.

★ Write in the smallest heart.

★ Punch red stars and glue them randomly over the page.

Star punch by Fiskars; computer font is Fontastic by DJ Inkers; calligraphy pen from the Zig Memory System; mounting tape by Therm O Web

BELLS.....

BELLS RING OUT AT CHRISTMAS OR FOR A WEDDING — THIS TEMPLATE IS IDEAL FOR EITHER.

CHRISTMAS BELLS

★ Photocopy the template opposite onto ivory paper. Colour in the artwork using brush pens.

★ Double matt the photographs with contrasting papers (see page 19). Trim the corners with a corner edger, if desired.

★ Glue the picture and matts onto the page.

Pens by Marvy Uchida and Royal Sovereign; Mono Adhesive by Tombow

Brush pens from the Marvy Memory Series by Marvy Uchida from Royal Sovereign; Mono Adhesive by Tombow

GOLDEN WEDDING BELLS

★ Photocopy the template opposite onto white paper. Colour in the artwork using brush pens.

★ Cut and fit single matts behind the photos (see page 19). Draw a gold line around the edge of each photo to highlight it. Glue the pictures and matts on the page.

★ Add captions and any journaling.

HEARTS ......

ONE PATTERN, TWO DIFFERENT LOOKS TO CELEBRATE TWO DIFFERENT EVENTS.

TEENAGE LOVE

★ *Photocopy the template onto coloured paper.*

★ *Cut out the heart shapes to form openings for your photos – leaving a slight margin, as here, enables you to take advantage of the black outline.*

★ *Place your photos behind the openings and trim away the excess.*

★ *Add the title or any other information you wish.*

★ *Draw the phone coils on coloured paper with a black scroll-tip pen.*

★ *Colour the edges with selected pencils or markers. Trim away the excess carefully and glue in place.*

Paper by Hot Off the Press

Corner rounder by Marvy Uchida; calligraphy pens from the Zig Memory System

NEW-BORN BABY

★ *Photocopy the template opposite onto white paper.*

★ *Use a wide calligraphy pen to draw overlapping strokes around the lower heart. Carefully cut away the heart shapes to form openings.*

★ *Colour in the open hearts on the background.*

★ *Trim the template border, cutting away the outside edge, then shape the corners with a rounded corner edger.*

★ *Place your photo behind the upper opening, trim away the excess and add a ribbon bow, if desired. Write the birth announcement on white paper and slip it behind the lower opening.*

★ *Colour the edge of white paper; centre your decorated page on top.*

ℬALLOONS ....

Balloons can mark any celebration, so you can use this template in many ways. Here are two ideas.

PLANET HOLLYWOOD CELEBRATION

★ Photocopy the template opposite onto white paper. Colour in the small pieces of confetti, the bow and the streamers.

★ Trim the edges of the photocopied sheet and mount it on decorative paper.

★ Crop your photos to fit into the balloons. Glue them on and outline them with a thick black marker for definition.

★ Crop your other photos as desired. We placed a matt under the small oval photo so it would stand out against the others. Glue these to the page.

★ Add your captions and journaling.

Paper © Dianne J Hook; pens from the Zig Memory System; Mono Adhesive by Tombow

Pencils by Derwent

CLOWNS

★ Photocopy the template. Cut out the balloons and photocopy them onto grey paper; colour them in.

★ Trim the picture around the balloons and glue it to the page.

★ Add suitable stickers randomly around the page and overlap some onto the photograph, if desired.

★ Add your caption.

BASIC SHAPES & CLIP ART

HERE ARE SOME BASIC SHAPES YOU CAN USE TO MAKE TEMPLATES TO CUT YOUR PHOTOS INTO UNUSUAL SHAPES PLUS THE CLIP ART WHICH IS USED EXTENSIVELY ON OUR ALBUM PAGES. ALL THE CLIP ART IS NUMBERED AND GROUPED INTO THEMES TO HELP YOU FIND THE RIGHT MOTIF FOR THE TYPE OF LAYOUT YOU ARE CREATING.

Many of the most striking album pages in this book are created by cutting the feature photos and their matts into special shapes, like the eye-catching stars in Baby Aaron (page 48) and you can do the same with the text. To help you get started you'll find some hearts, stars, ovals and other shapes here, but you can also buy or make your own templates if you prefer.

To use the basic shapes first enlarge or reduce them, if necessary, on a photocopier, then trace them onto a sheet of acrylic and cut them out, following the instructions on page 31. When you want to cut a photo or matt to shape, simply lay your template on top and draw round the shape. Carefully cut out the shape along the drawn line.

USING THE CLIP ART

There are two ways of using the clip art. The easiest method is to photocopy the items you want, colour them in with felt-tip pens or coloured pencils as desired and then cut them out and glue them in position on your page.

The second option is to make a guide. This enables you to photocopy the motifs in position directly onto your background paper for a more integrated look. To do this, first copy the appropriate clip art and cut it out. Glue it onto a sheet of white paper in the position required to make the guide. Load the photocopier with your background paper and then photocopy the guide onto this. (See page 35 for further details.)

BASIC SHAPES & PATTERNS

NAPPY TEMPLATE FROM PAGE 48

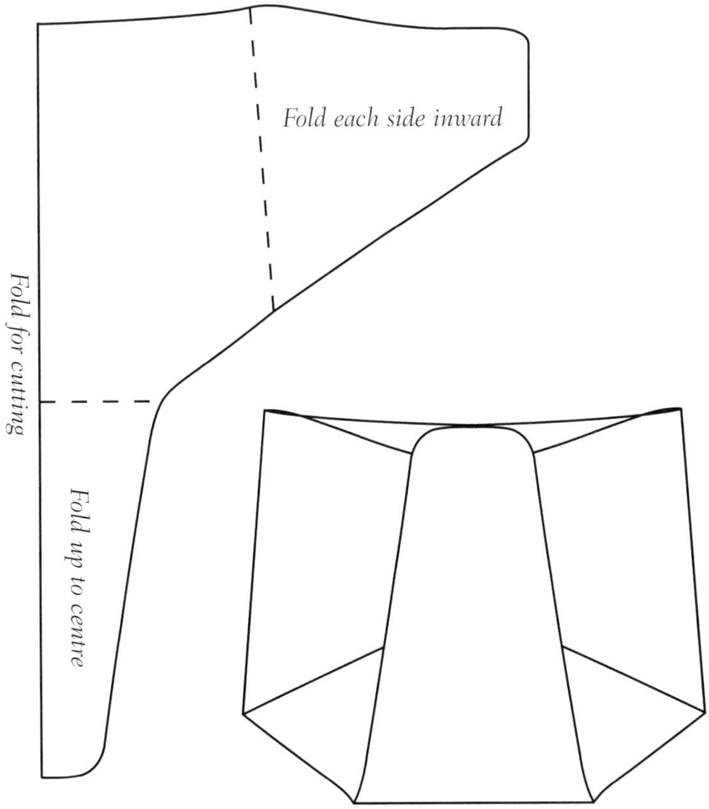

Fold each side inward

Fold for cutting

Fold up to centre

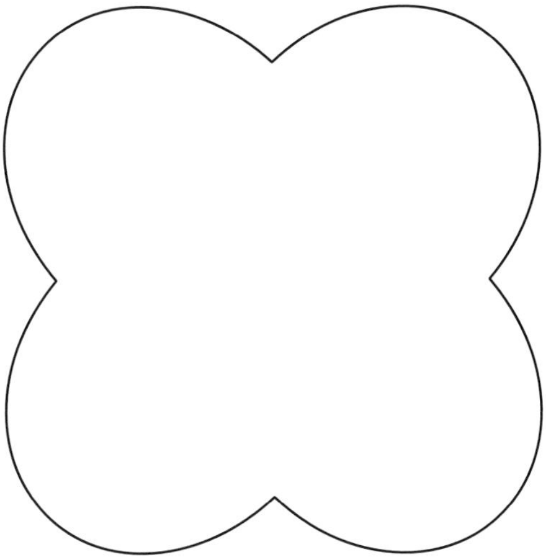

KEEPER ENVELOPE TEMPLATE
FROM PAGE 37

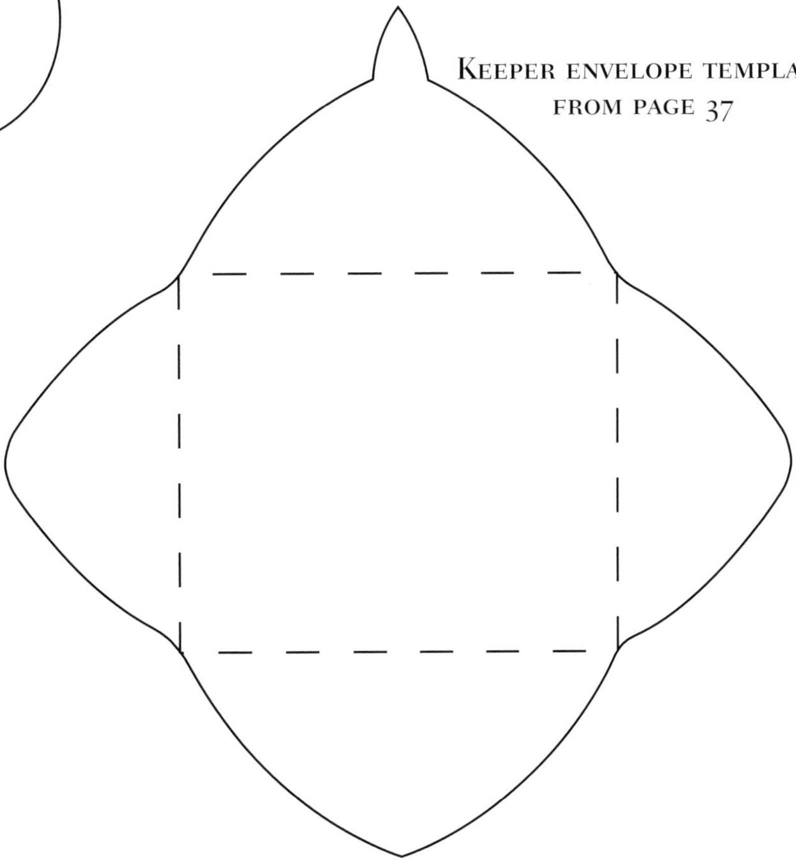

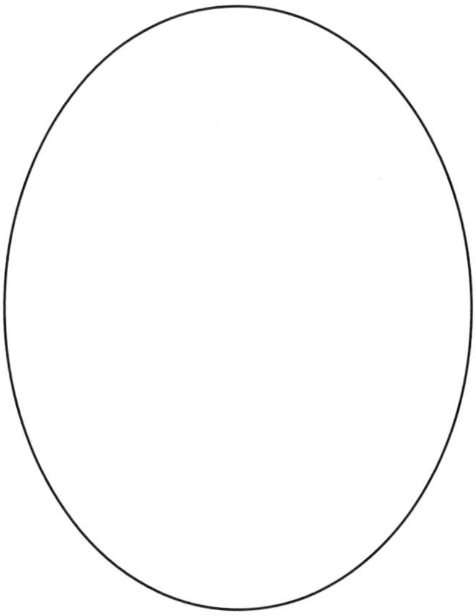

CLIP ART

15

16

17

18

19

20

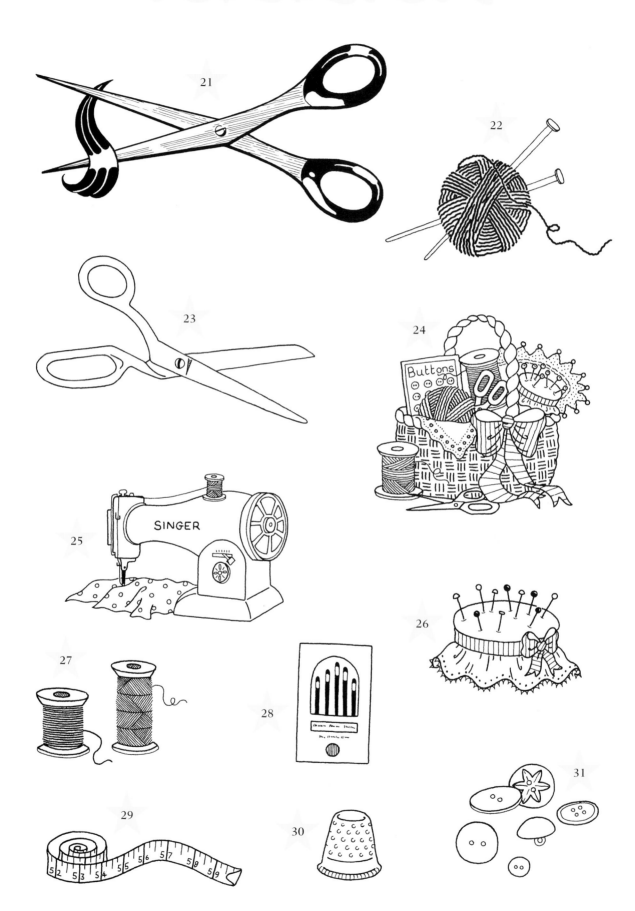

42

43

44

45

ZOEY

46

47

48

49

50

51

52

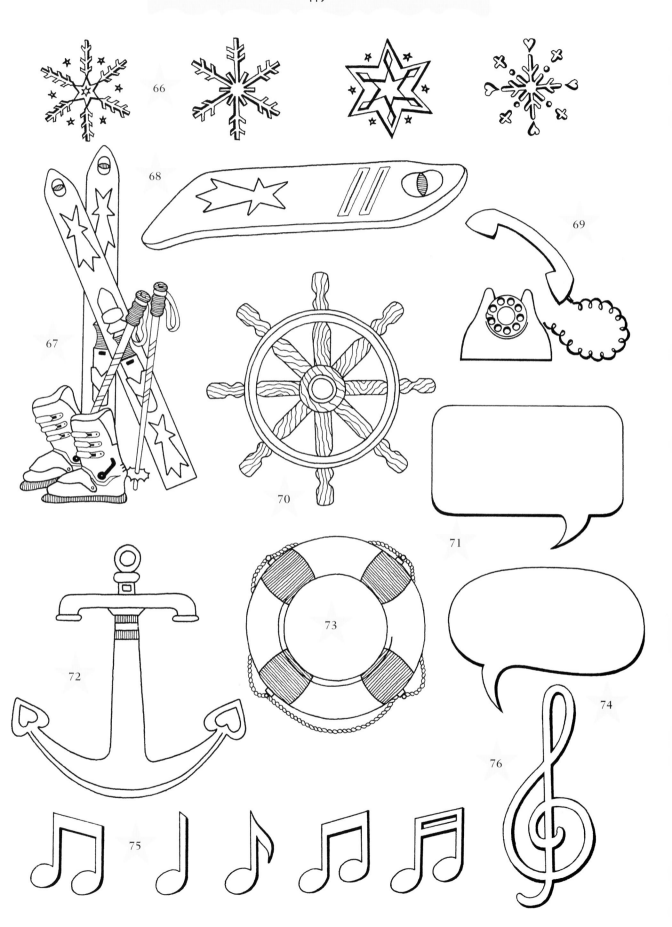

83

84

82

86

85

87

88

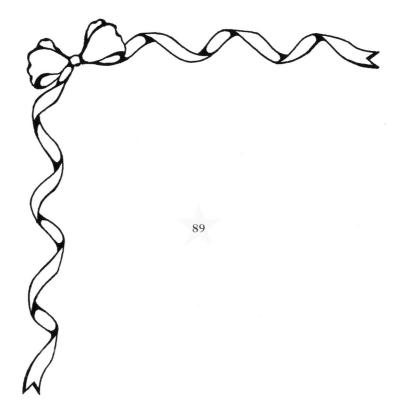

89

Alphabets

A a B b C c D d E e F f

G g H h I i J j K k L l

M m N n O o P p Q q

R r S s T t U u V v

W w X x Y y Z z

1

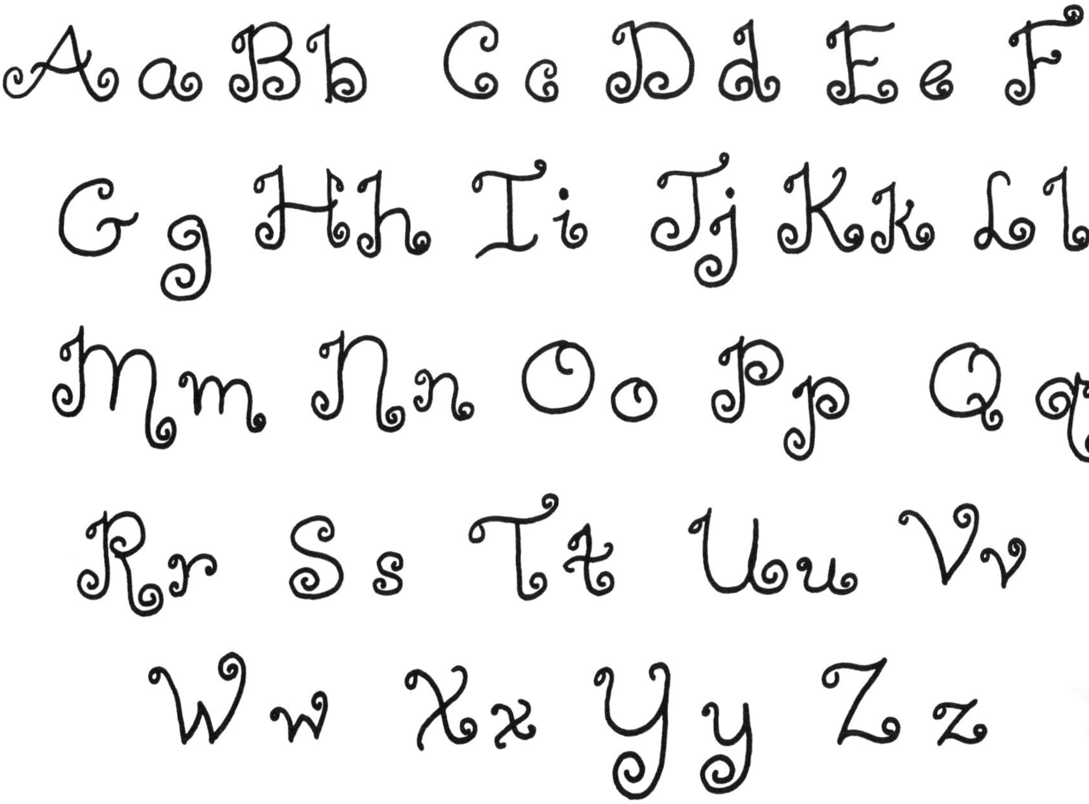

Aa Bb Cc Dd Ee Ff
Gg Hh Ii Jj Kk Ll
Mm Nn Oo Pp Qq
Rr Ss Tt Uu Vv
Ww Xx Yy Zz   2

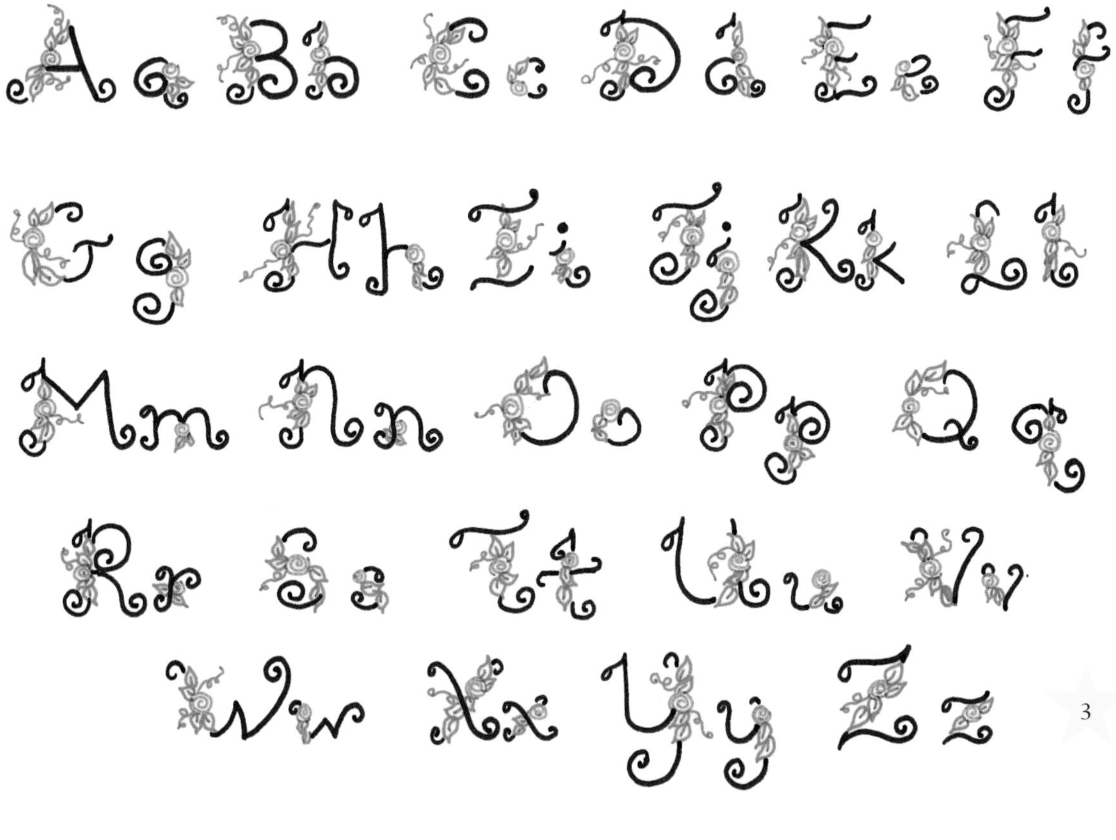

Aa Bb Cc Dd Ee Ff
Gg Hh Ii Jj Kk Ll
Mm Nn Oo Pp Qq
Rr Ss Tt Uu Vv
Ww Xx Yy Zz   3

SUPPLIERS

UK MANUFACTURERS AND DISTRIBUTORS

COLART CRAFT NETWORK
(kits, paper and page protectors)
Whitefriars Avenue,
Wealdstone, Harrow,
Middx. HA3 5RH
Tel: 0181 427 4343
Fax: 0181 863 7177

THE CRAFT BARN
9 East Grinstead Road,
Lingfield, Surrey RH7 6EP
Tel: 01342 832 977
Fax: 01342 835 792

FIRST CLASS STAMPS LTD
(UK & European distributor for All Night Media; wide range of memory album products)
1 George Edwards Road,
Fakenham, Norfolk
NR21 9NJ
Tel: 01328 851 449
Fax: 01328 864 828

KURETAKE UK LTD (Zig Memory System, pens)
10 Moons Park, Burnt Meadow Road, Redditch, Worcestershire B98 9PA
Tel: 01527 62828
Fax: 01527 60765

PERSONAL IMPRESSIONS
(stamps, cutting tools, templates and rulers)
Curzon Road, Chilton Industrial Estate,
Sudbury, Suffolk CO10 6XW
Tel: 01787 375 241
Fax: 01787 310 179

PRIORITY SOURCING
INTERNATIONAL (exclusive UK and European distributors for Accu-Cut, Ravishing Wraps, Creating Keepsakes magazine,
Xyron machines and other memory supplies)
Tel: 07970 924 440

ROYAL SOVEREIGN LTD.
(Uniball pens, ink and paint)
Units 6/7, St George's Industrial Estate,
Whitehart Lane,
London N22 5QL
Tel: 0181 888 6888
Fax: 0181 888 7029

UK RETAILERS AND MAIL-ORDER COMPANIES

ARTBASE (mail order)
88 North Street,
Hornchurch, Essex RM11 1SR
Tel: 01708 457 948
Fax: 01708 457949

ARTBASE (mail order)
514 Brompton Walk,
Lakeside Shopping Centre, West Thurrock,
Essex RM20 2ZL
Tel: 01708 865 330

C & H FABRICS
(Brighton)
Tel: 01273 321 959

C & H FABRICS
(Canterbury)
Tel: 01227 459 760

THE CRAFT BARN
(mail order)
9 East Grinstead Road,
Lingfield, Surrey
RH7 6EP
Tel: 01342 832 977
Fax: 01342 835 792

CRAFT KINGDOM
(Hereford)
Tel: 01432 264 800

MILLERS CITY ART SHOP
(Glasgow)
Tel: 0141 553 1660

MOMENTS OF MAGIC LTD
(mail order)
64 Erica Way, Capthorne
W.S. RH10 3XQ
Tel: 01343 718898
Fax: 01342 717469

THE STAMP MAN
(Skipton)
Tel: 01756 797 048

USA MANUFACTURERS AND DISTRIBUTORS

ACCU-CUT
(die cuts)
1035 E Dodge,
PO Box 1053,
Fremont, NE 68025
Tel: (800) 288 1670 / (402) 721 8185
Fax: (402) 721-5778
E-mail: info@accucut.com
Website: //www.accucut.com

AMERICAN TRADITIONAL
STENCILS
(stencils)
442 First New Hampshire Turnpike, Northwood,
NH 03261
Tel: (603) 942 8100 / (800) 448 6656
Fax: (603) 942 8919 / (800) 448 6654
Website: www.amtrad-stencil.com

API, THE ADHESIVE
PRODUCTS, INC
(adhesives)
520 Cleveland Avenue,
Albany,
CA 94710
Tel: (510) 526 7616
Fax: (510) 524 0573

ART 2 ART
(mail order)
PO Box 8370,
Springfield, MO 65801
USA
Tel: 800 284 8195
Fax: 800 284 8216
Website: www.art2art.net

BLUMENTHAL LANSING
(kits)
One Palmer Terrace,
Carlstadt, NJ 07072
Tel: (800) 448 9749
Fax: (201) 935 0055

CANSON-TALENS INC
South Hadley, MA 01075
Tel: (800) 628 9283

CENTURY CRAFT
(albums, page protectors, kits)
205 S Puente, Brea, CA 92662
Tel: (714) 441 4500 / (800) 340 2031
Fax: (714) 441 4550

C-LINE PRODUCTS, INC
(page protectors)
Tel: (800) 323-6084

C-THRU RULER COMPANY
(templates, fancy rulers and stencils)
6 Britton Drive, Box 356,
Bloomfield, CT 06002
Tel: 860 242 0303
Fax: 860 243 1856
E-mail: ccthru@aol.com

CREATIVE PAPERS BY C.R.
GIBSON (paper)
32 Knight Street,
Norwalk, CT. 06856

CUT IT UP (books)
4543 Orange Grove Ave,
Sacramento, CA 95841
Tel: (916) 482 2288
Fax: (916) 482 1331

CREATING KEEPSAKES
SCRAPBOOK MAGAZINE
PO Box 1106,
Orem,
UT 84059-9956
Tel: 801 224 8235
Fax: 801 947 1537

DAISY KINGDOM
(fabric)
134 NW 8th Ave,
Portland, OR 97209
Tel: (503) 222 9033
Fax: (503) 224 8566

DELTA
(paint)
2550 Pellissier Place,
Whittier, CA 90601
Website:http://www.deltacrafts.com

DESIGN ORIGINALS
(paper, books and stickers)
2425 Cullen St, Ft
Worth, Texas 76107
Tel: (817) 877 0067/(800)
877 7820
Fax: (817) 877 0861

DJ INKERS
(computer software, paper,
stamps and stickers)
PO Box 2462, Sandy, UT 84091
Tel: (801) 944-4680
Fax: (801) 944-0475
E-mail:
djcorp@djinkers.com
Web page: www.djinkers.com

D.O.T.S.
(stamps)
Tel: (888) 655 6552
Fax: (801) 763 8188

EK SUCCESS
(Zig Memory System pens
and books)
PO Box 6507, Carlstadt,
NJ 07072-6507
Tel: (800) 524 1349 /
(201) 939 5404
Fax: (800) 767 2963 /
(201) 939 4511

ELLISON CRAFT & DESIGN
(die cuts and books)
17171 Daimler St, Irvine,
CA 92614
Tel: (888) 972 7238
Fax: (888) 270 1200

FAMILY TREASURES
(scissors, punches, die
cuts, rulers and books)
Tel: (800) 413 2645
Fax: (800) 891 3520

FISKARS, INC
(scissors, punches, albums
and more)
7811 W Stewart Ave,
Wausau, WI 54401
Tel: (800) 950 0203
E-mail: hhttp://www.fiskars.com

FRANCES MEYER INC
(stickers)
Tel: (800) FRANCES

THE GIFTED LINE
(stickers)
Tel: (800) 5 GIFTED

**MRS. GROSSMAN'S PAPER
CO** (stickers)
3810 Cypress Dr.,
Petaluma, CA 94954
Tel: (707) 763 1700 /
(800) 429 4549
Fax: (707) 763 7121
E-mail: mgpc@mrsgross-
mans.com
Web page: www.mrsgross-
man.com

HILLER
(albums)
631 North 400 West, Salt
Lake City, UT 84103
Tel: (801) 521 2411
Fax: (801) 521 2420

HOT OFF THE PRESS
(paper and books)
1250 NW Third, Canby,
OR 97013
Tel: (503) 266 9102
Fax: 503 266 8749

HYGLOSS PRODUCTS INC.
(paper)
402 Broadway, Passaic,
NJ 07055
Tel: (201) 458 1700
Fax: (201) 458 1745

**INTERNATIONAL
SCRAPBOOK TRADE
ASSOCIATION**
(information)
PO Box 295250,
Lewisville,
TX 75029-5250
Tel: (972) 318 0492
Fax: (972) 318 0491

RA LANG
(stickers)
Tel: 414 646 2388

LIGHT IMPRESSIONS
(preservation supplies)
439 Monroe Ave,
PO Box 940,
Rochester
NY 14603-0940
Tel: (800) 828 6216 /
(716) 271 8960

MAKING MEMORIES
(stickers)
PO Box 1188,
Centerville, UT 84014
1-800-286-5263

MARK ENTERPRISES
(stickers)
PO Box 3094, Newport
Beach, CA 92659
Tel: (714) 631 9200
Fax: (714) 631 1244

MARVY UCHIDA
(pens, punches and stamps)
Uchida of America Corp.
3535 Del Amo Blvd,
Torrance, CA 90503
Tel: (310) 793 2200 /
(800) 541 5877
Fax: (800) 229 7017

MBI THE ALBUM PEOPLE
Somerset, NJ 08873

MCGILL, INC
(punches)
131 E Prairie St,
Marengo, IL 60152
Tel: (800) 982 9884

MELISSA NEUFELD, INC.
(stickers)
7068 Koll Center Pkwy.,
Suite 425, Pleasanton,
CA 94566
Tel: 1 800 638 3353
Fax: (510) 417 0755
Web site: www.melissa-
neufeld.com

MPR ASSOC. INC.
(paper)
PO Box 7343
High Point, NC 27264
Tel: (910) 861 6343
Fax: (910) 861 6393

NRN DESIGNS
(stickers, paper and kits)
Tel: (800) 421 6985
Fax: (800) 898 0015

THE PAPER PATCH
(paper)
PO Box 414, Riverton,
Utah 84065
Tel: (800) 397 2737 /
253 3018
Fax: (801) 253 3019

**PERSONAL STAMP
EXCHANGE** (stamps)
360 Sutton Place, Santa
Rosa, CA 95407
Tel: (707) 588 8058
Fax: (707) 588 7476

**PIONEER PHOTO
ALBUMS INC**
(albums)
9801 Deering Avenue,
Chatsworth, CA 91311
Tel: 818 882 2161 / (800)
366-3686
Fax: 818 882 6239
E-mail: pioneer@pioneer-
photoalbums.com

PLAID ENTERPRISES INC.
(FolkArt acrylic paint and
stencils)
1649 International Court,
Norcross, Georgia 30093
Tel: 770 923 8200
Fax: 770 717 3145

PROVO CRAFT
(paper, stickers and com-
puter software)
285 E 900 S, Provo,
UT 84606
Tel: (801) 377 4311 /
(800) 937 7686
Fax: (801) 373 1901

REMEMBER WHEN...
(kits, die cuts and stickers)
Tel: (510) 938 1700

ROCKY MOUNTAIN CRAFT
540 E 500 North
American Fork, Utah
84003-1976
Tel: (801) 763 8628
Fax: (801) 756 0577

SAKURA OF AMERICA
(pens)
30780 San Clemente St,
Hayward CA 94544
Tel: 800 776-6257

STAMP DEVILLE
(stamps)
1014 S Broadaway Suite
100, Carrollton,
Texas 75006
Tel: (800) 247 1893 /
(972) 245 5755

STAMPENDOUS
(stamps)
Tel: (714) 563 9501 /
(800) 869 0474
Fax: (714) 563 9509 /
(800) 578 2FAX
Web: http://www.stamp-
endous.com

STICKOPOTAMUS INC
(stickers)
PO Box 86,
Carlstadt,
NJ 07072-0086
Tel: (201) 939 5404
Fax: (201) 939 4511

STRATHMORE PAPER C. /
INTERNATIONAL PAPER
(paper)
39 South Broad St,
Westfield, MA 01085
Tel: (413) 572 9242
Tel: (413) 572 9240

THERM O WEB
(adhesives, paper, calendars and kits)
770 Glenn Avenue,
Wheeling, IL 60090
Tel: (800) 323 0799

TSUKINEKO
(pigment ink)
15411 NE 95th Street,
Redmond, WA 98052,
USA
Tel: (206) 883 7733 /
(800) 769 6633
Fax: (206) 883 7418

WALNUT HOLLOW
(albums)
1409 State Rd 23,
Dodgeville, WI 53533
Tel: (608) 935 2341
Fax: (608) 935 3029

USA RETAILERS AND MAIL-ORDER COMPANIES

ALWAYS & FOREVER
(mail order only)
220 W Grand Ave,
El Segundo,
CA 90245
Tel: 310 322 9571
Fax: 310 322 9573
Website: www.scrapper-stidbits.com

AN ANGEL'S ART
(St Paul, MN)
Tel: 612 646 6477

ARTFULLY SCRIBED
(Herndon, VA)
Tel: 703 78 STAMP

ARTISTIC ALBUMS & MORE
(mail order only)
PO Box 5123-416, El
Toro, CA 92630
Tel: 888 9 ALBUMS

CALLIGRAPHY HOUSE
(Piedmont, SC)
Tel: 864 295 9111

CAROLINA ART STAMPS
(Matthews, NC)
Tel: 704 841 2600

COCO STAMP
(San Francisco, CA)
Tel: 415 566 1018

COUNTRY CREATIONS
(Knowville, TN)
Tel: 423 675 5668

COUNTRY IMAGES
(Ocala, FL)
Tel: 352 237 5411

COUNTRY NEEDLEWORKS
(Jenison, MI)
Tel: 616 457 9410

COWTOWN STAMP-EDE
(Vacaville, CA)
Tel: 707 446 7256

CREATE AN IMPRESSION
(Ardmore, PA)
Tel: 610 645 6500

CREATIVE IMPRESSIONS,
RUBBER STAMPS INC.
(Colorado Springs, CO)
Tel: 719 577 4858

CREATIVE PALS
(Brookfield, WI)
Tel: 414 938 5959

CROPPIN' CONNECTION
(Bartlett, TN)
Tel: 901 388 8803

DERBY CITY STAMPING
COMPANY (Louisville, KY)
Tel: 502 895 0FUN

ENCHANTED COTTAGE
(Lewisville, NC)
Tel: 910 945 5889

ECCENTRICITIES
(Spring TX)
Tel: 281 288 0585

FAMILY BASE
Tel: (888) 327-6472
Website: www.family-base.com

FAMILY TREE SCRAPBOOK
SUPPLIES
Tel: (604) 859 8970

FROM THE HEART
(Claremont, CA)
Tel: 909 626 3479

HANDCRAFT HOUSE
(Madison, VA)
Tel: 540 948 6323

HETHERINGTON
SPECIALTIES
(Hobart, OK0)
Tel: 580 726 6613

IMPRESS YOURSELF
(Jacksonville, FL)
Tel: 904 260 7759

IMPRESS YOURSELF
(Prior Lake, MN)
Tel: 612 496 3380

KEEP STAMPIN' LTD
(Berkley, MI)
Tel 248 544 7322

LIGHTHOUSE
SCRAPBOOKING
(Salem, NH)
Tel: 603 870 9222

MEMORIES
Tel: 800 929 7324
Website:
www.memories.com

MEMORIES TO CHERISH
(mail order)
Memorybook Lane,
Naperville, IL
Tel: 630 416 4300

PAPER POTPOURRI
(Lakeland, FL)
Tel: 941 853 1492

THE PAPER RABBIT
(Montrose, CA)
Tel: (818) 957 2848

THE PAPER RABBIT
(Valencia, CA)
Tel: (805) 287 9283

PAPER REFLECTIONS
(DMD Ind) (mail order)
1205 ESI Drive,
Springdale, AR 72764
Tel: (800) 805 9890
Website: www.dmdind.com

PARTY ADVENTURES
(Palm Dessert, CA)
Tel: 760 341 2339

PEBBLES IN MY POCKET
(mail order)
PO Box 1506, Orem,
Utah 84059-4835 USA
Tel: (800) 438 8153
Fax: (801) 223 4835
E-mail: pebbles@pebblesinmypocket.com
Website: http://www.pebblesinmypocket.com

PHOTOGRAPHIC MEMORIES
(Liberty, MO)
Tel: 816 415 9003

PLANET RUBBER
(Clearwater, FL)
Tel: 813 669 4114

REMEMBER THE MOMENT
(Geneva, IL)
Tel: 630 232 8715

ROCKY MOUNTAIN CRAFT
(mail order)
540 East 500 North American
Fork, UT 84003-1976
Tel: (801) 763 8628 /
(800) 270 9130
Fax: (801) 756 0577
Website: http:www.rmcraft.com

RUBBER AGE STAMPS
(Parma, OK)
Tel: 216 398 7001

THE RUBBER ROOM
(Medina, OH)
Tel: 330 722 2863

THE RUBBER STAMP LADY
(Huntsville, AL)
Tel: 205 880 1106

SCRAPBOOKS 'N MORE
(mail order)
5769 Westcreek, Ft
Worth, TX 76133
Tel: 888 312 4449
Website: www.scrapbook-snmore.com

THE SCRAPBOOK COMPANY (mail order)
1115 North 200 East, Suite 140, Logan, Utah 84341
Tel: (888) 750 6844
E-mail: info@scrapbook-company.com
Website: www.scrapbook-company.com

SCRAPBOOK INSPIRATIONS
(Springfield, IL)
Tel: 217 241 5900

THE SCRAPBOOK LADY
(Canton Centre, CT)
Tel: 860 693 9197

SIMPLE PLEASURES
(Colorado Springs, CO)
Tel: 719 528 1338

THE SCRAPBOOK CONNECTION
(West Linn, OR)
Tel: 503 656 2426

THE SCRAPBOOK STORE
(West Allis, WI)
Tel: 414 545 9545

THE SCRAPBOOK STORY
(Rancho Cucamonga, CA)
Tel: 909 944 3305

SCRAPBOOKS UNLIMITED
(mail order)
Tel: (602) 610 0092
Fax: (602) 844 9003

SCRAPPERS
(Meridian, ID)
Tel: 208 887 9311

SCRAPPERS UNLIMITED
(mail order)
PO Box 337, Eureka, Missouri 63025
E-mail: info@scrappers.com

STAMP-A-DOODLE
(Bellingham WA)
Tel: 360 647 9663

STAMP DEVILLE
(Carrollton, TX)
Tel: (972) 245-5755 / (800) 247 1893

THE STAMPER'S EMPORIUM
(Sparta, NJ)
Tel: 201 729 8787

STAMPER'S PARADISE
(Virginia Beach, VA)

STAMPFASTIC
(Gurnee, IL)
Tel: 847 855 1050

STAMPFASTIC
(Kenosha, WI)
Tel: 414 697 7697

STAMP HEAVEN CRAFT
(Hilton Head, SC)
Tel: 803 686 3932

STAMPIN' GROUNDS
(Goose Creek, SC)
Tel: 803 797 8366

THE STAMPING PLACE
(Columbia, SC)
Tel: 803 791 1440

STAMPS 'N' SCRAPS A GIFT FOR A FRIEND
(Middlebury, IN)
Tel: 219 825 5129

STAMP STREET STATION
(Sarasota, FL)
Tel: 941 927 2667

STAMPING WILD
(Plantation, FL)
Tel: 954 584 8111

STAMP YOUR ART OUT
(Cincinnati, OH)
Tel: 513 793 4558

TAMP-A-STAMP
(Tampa, FL)
Tel: 813 258 8682

MRS. VA'S PHOTO DESIGNS
(mail order)
142 Miller Drive, Naugatuck, CT 06770-2207
Tel: 203 723 5484
Fax: 203 723 6961
E-mail: MrsVAphoto@aol.com

THE VILLAGE SCRIBE SHOPPE (Santa Claus, IN)
Tel: 812 937 4590

WONDERLAND EMPORIUM
(Delray Beach, FL)
Tel: 561 276 7116

ℰ𝒜CKNOWLEDGEMENTS

Many thanks to the following people for sharing their treasured photos with us as well as those who were the photographic subjects.

Christy Abadilla, Bertha Alves, Kay Anderson, Michael, Suzie, Megan and Ben Azevedo, Chuck and Suzanne Bell, Bishopsteignton Cubs Football Team, John and Beverley Boogaard and grandchildren, Rose Briner, Cheryl Brown, Frances Cavanagh, Dean Collins, Janet Cooper, Dorois Cox, Helen Cox, Richard, Lisa, Sarah, Ian and Hannah Donkin, Harry Duns, Bob, Kathy, Heidi, Michael and Steven Ekema, John and Tina Ekema, Lynne Farris, Brian and Pauline Fell, Muhamed, Enisa and Demir Filipovic, Merrima, Emir and Emina Filipovic, Bill, Terri and Aly Fishbough, Anne and Shaun Flynn, Lois and Michael Foley, Bill and Amelia Garcia, Hertingfordbury Cowper JMI A Football Team, 1996/7, Dave McGann, Graeme Mills, Joe Mills, John Mills, Sally Mills, Stephen Mills, Hannah Mills-Brown, Joe Mills-Brown, Brenda Morrison, Carol Nelson, Jim and Sue Parks, Justin and Jarrod Perreria, Vivian Perrits, Rosie Ramirez, Kathy Sanders, Christopher Schulz, Viktor and Dana Schulz, Mark Schulz, Richard Schulz, Tony Schulz, Susan Simas, Janice Slowey, Ida Souza, Carl E. and Dellores Smith, Carl F. and Maude Smith, Julie Stephani, Mr Tomasa, Gavin and Deborah Trott, Aaron Vertrees, Bernard and Wanda Vertrees, Leanne Vertrees, Grace and Rusty Wakugawa, Durwyn and Frieda Wild and family, Louis and Inez Wright, Marion and Chris Wright, Arthur Zeismer.